T0278990

WALKING SOUTH CITY

A JOURNEY THROUGH HISTORIC ST. LOUIS NEIGHBORHOODS

Visit Jim Merkel at jimmerkelthewriter.com.

Library of Congress Control Number: 2023931749

ISBN: 9781681064390

Cover photo by Joseph Puleo.

Interior photos courtesy of K.L. Droney and B. Northcott unless otherwise noted.

Printed in the United States of America
23 24 25 26 27 5 4 3

WALKING SOUTH CITY

A JOURNEY THROUGH HISTORIC ST. LOUIS NEIGHBORHOODS

JIM MERKEL

Lafayette Park House

CONTENTS

PREFACE

This book began with an eight-mile walk that my publisher, Josh Stevens, took with his twelve-year-old son in the depths of the COVID-19 pandemic. The trek from their house in the Lindenwood Park neighborhood to the Gateway Arch in the summer of 2020 gave them a taste of neighborhoods like The Hill, Lafayette Square, LaSalle, and Downtown. It confirmed why they love St. Louis. On a different day, they walked about the same distance to Kirkwood, but it wasn't the same. They discovered the county had fewer sidewalks, heavier traffic, and was generally more difficult to navigate on foot than the city.

The experience inspired Josh to propose an idea to me in early 2021. With CDC guidelines still recommending physical distancing, we decided to meet on the heated patio at Annex Coffee and Foods in Webster Groves' Old Orchard. The heaters were on full blast, but we still felt a chill. I warmed up when I heard his idea about writing a book on walks through the neighborhoods of South St. Louis. The proposal was too good to ignore and led to the volume you're reading, which recounts what I witnessed and learned during my 45-cumulative-mile stroll through South St. Louis, known more commonly these days as South City.

Before embarking on my journey, I read Bill Bryson's *A Walk in the Woods: Rediscovering America on the Appalachian Trail* for inspiration and perspective. *A Walk in the Woods* is a funny but poignant travelogue about the author's experience hiking across the eastern states. The book is a howler but describes the trail as well as any serious book, and Bryson ties in his relationships with his family and walking partner (I brought along people for my walks, too).

This book attempts to capture South City in a similar way. It's the second I've written about the lower half of St. Louis. The first,

Hoosiers and Scrubby Dutch, became a local favorite and led to other books for Reedy Press on topics like the area's German American community, the Gateway Arch, the city's quirky characters, and the experience of growing up in St. Louis.

Fortunately, with this project, my knowledge of the covered area was strong. My German great-great grandfather settled with his family in South City in 1858. My brother represents the fifth generation in the piano business in St. Louis. I've lived in the Bevo Mill neighborhood with my wife, Lorraine, for more than 30 years, and I reported on this part of town for the old *South Side Journal* from 2001 to 2009.

In our discussions about a new concept, Josh and I decided it wouldn't be a typical collection of short essays about neighborhoods, people, and events. Instead, we wanted the book to provide a living perspective. I planned to include conversations with people I encountered along the walks, from leaders of the community to people walking their dogs. I would incorporate neighborhood history, but my biggest focus would be what I saw, from the immaculately restored and preserved homes of Lafayette Square to the factories and empty storefronts of South Broadway in Carondelet.

The walking route herein touches all of South City's neighborhoods. The result was a winding path that stays south of Highway 40. This book divides the route into 17 walks that range from 1.5 to 4 miles. A caution: the tours in this book don't take you down every street. We left out some important territory. The River des Peres Greenway, for example, offers some nature in the middle of the city and an entryway to the much larger Great Rivers Greenway. We also leave out much of Arsenal Street, which passes the Anheuser-Busch brewery and Benton Park. Readers might consider exploring both walks on their own.

During the walks, I kept my eyes open for details, noting everything from a run-down house to a discarded surgical mask commonly worn during the pandemic. I looked for the oddities, serious and humorous. For instance, the head of a statue of a mouse in the Grove leans heavily in one direction—an indication that the leaders of the Grove don't take themselves seriously. As I sought the unusual, I recorded my own observations and reflections.

By the time I sat down to write, I had collected hundreds of impressions about South City. Hopefully, the final product offers an authentic view of an authentic place. It's hard to believe the whole thing started with a walk to the Arch in the midst of a pandemic.

Thomas Hart Benton statue
in Lafayette Park

PROLOGUE

There was a railroad but not just any railroad. Civic leaders who started laying the rails for this line wanted it to stretch not only west but all the way to the Pacific Ocean. Early backers of a railroad to the Pacific included US Senator Thomas Hart Benton, who represented Missouri for three decades after it became a state in 1821. Benton said at an 1849 meeting in St. Louis that a transcontinental railroad to San Francisco would help the US dominate trade in the Far East. You'll find his quote, "There is the East. There is India," inscribed at the base of his statue, dedicated in 1868 and standing tall in Lafayette Park. Benton forever faces west wearing explorer boots and the toga of a Roman senator.

The railroad never made it to San Francisco, but it did have a major effect nationally and locally. It's one of many acts of individuals and nature that influenced the part of town I walked from January to December 2021. Discovering these acts would cause any observant walker to say, "Would you look at that?"

Inspired by Benton, St. Louisans who backed that railroad started building the line west from the center of downtown in the early 1850s. The path of the new railroad to the Pacific traversed land just south of present-day Manchester Avenue. The line helped the economy but not the South Side. Historians generally say the railroads, along with the Mill Creek Valley, blocked access to South St. Louis. Access improved in 1889, with the construction of the Grand Avenue Viaduct over the westward railroad tracks and Mill Creek Valley. Other north-south bridges also reduced the sense of isolation, but the damage was already done. City maps published at the start of the 20th century show that much of southwestern St. Louis was empty.

Most believe that story, but not Chris Naffziger. He's an archives researcher for St. Louis and operates the Saint Louis Patina website. He doesn't think the lack of viaducts or the presence of train tracks stunted north-south traffic, and streetcars did go from north to south. What he does believe slowed down construction in South St. Louis is the land itself. Sinkholes are common, and builders need huge amounts of dirt to fill them in. The topography, made of limestone and referred to as *karst*, is full of caves, holes, and underground streams. In serious cases, it may cause a house to lean or collapse. The South Side, unlike the North Side, is hilly, which also presents construction challenges. According to Naffziger, straight streets go on forever in the North Side.

The South Side may have grown slowly, but that wasn't necessarily bad. When development began in earnest west of Kingshighway, the housing style was more suburban and modern. The delay increased the variety of neighborhoods on the South Side. St. Louis Hills was the Chesterfield of the time. (What a joy it was to look at those English-style homes as I walked next to Francis Park.) And it's all possible because of a dammed creek, some railroad tracks, and a dearth of good bridges. Had all of the South Side developed earlier, the houses in St. Louis Hills might have looked like the two-story red-brick homes in southeast city.

That's not to criticize red-brick neighborhoods. Brick was a major force in the city even before the great riverfront fire in 1849 led the city to pass more ordinances requiring developers to incorporate brick. The city ranked among a handful of metropolises in the quality of its brick. Credit the South Side's rich clay deposits, plentiful in the ground just west of present-day Hampton Avenue between Oakland and Manchester Avenues. Italian immigrants working in the developing Hill neighborhoods and Irish immigrants in the Dogtown neighborhood and elsewhere toiled at a firebrick works in the area. The clay they mined could withstand the high temperatures needed to make a high-quality product. In much of southeast St. Louis, you'll find block after block of houses made of these bricks. They give parts of St. Louis a historic appearance that many other cities lack.

Besides the homes, trees between streets and sidewalks give a distinctive appearance to St. Louis neighborhoods. Without these trees, planted by the city's Forestry Division, St. Louis's streets would be barren and hot. Almost everywhere I sauntered in South City, the branches and leaves on either side meet toward the center of the streets. The 35 or so kinds of trees the Forestry Division makes available for planting include bald cypress, black gum, birch, cherry, various kinds of elms and maples, gingko, and hackberry. The city provided my wife and I with a sweet gum tree, which is stocky and full of thick leaves for much of the year. For a few months, it turns naked and ugly, with spikey balls constantly dropping to the ground. They can leave a mess if you don't rake them, however, my troubles don't make the whole system a failure. Almost everywhere I went in South City, the trees provided a canopy on hot days and granted me a deep drink of nature.

Speaking of nature, you'll find plenty of it in our parks. The most significant ones are the biggest, and they include Carondelet Park and Tower Grove Park. Other gems of varying sizes—Francis Park, Willmore Park, Lindenwood Park, Marquette Park, and Benton Park, for example—give a taste of the outdoors. So does the River des Peres Greenway, a green space that winds along the River des Peres to the Mississippi River. The greenway features a paved trail that stretches from a pocket park at Arsenal and McCausland to Carondelet and Lemay Parks.

In addition to parks, the prominence of the Catholic Church also stood out during my walks. Towering houses of worship add inspired architectural beauty to the neighborhoods they complement. The pinnacle of St. Francis de Sales Oratory lifts up what otherwise might be a drab stretch of Gravois. The smaller churches, schools, and other buildings I saw aren't so overwhelming, but they do draw the eye. The plans of the Archdiocese of St. Louis to close many of its buildings in 2023 promised to reduce this impact.

In some places, huge personalities have come forward to change the complexion of major parts of the South Side. One, Henry Shaw, was born in England in 1800, arrived in St. Louis in 1819, and began a career selling iron works, cutlery, and hardware. After 20 years, he gained so much wealth that he quit and focused on accumulating acreage west of downtown. As part of this effort, he built the Missouri Botanical Garden and Tower Grove Park, two masterworks that continue to enrich our city immeasurably. From the 1920s to the 1950s, Cyrus Crane Willmore turned about 700 acres of land at the southwestern edge of the city into a high-class suburb known as St. Louis Hills.

In the 1960s and 1970s, Washington University Chancellor William Danforth helped to revive major swaths of the St. Louis Central Corridor. While other hospitals were moving from the city to the county, Danforth campaigned to keep the Washington University Medical School and its affiliated hospitals where they were. Then Danforth decided to protect the medical center by making major investments in surrounding neighborhoods that included Forest Park Southeast, which includes the Grove, a thriving entertainment and residential district along Manchester Avenue east of Kingshighway.

It's easy to credit the work of giants for turning around a community, but everyday individuals with vision and conviction deserve their share, too. Such folks moved into struggling neighborhoods like Lafayette Square and Soulard, learned how to use a power saw, and revealed the original glory of those places.

It truly takes all kinds, including residents who diligently keep up their homes in the spirit of the old "Scrubby Dutch."

I encountered more than bright spots during my walks. Urban decay and population decline since World War II still afflicts areas of South City, especially southeast. One example is a vacant lot on the southeast corner of Chippewa Street and Morgan Ford Road, not far from my house. When Lorraine and I moved back to St. Louis from Pennsylvania in 1991, a Steak 'n Shake occupied the lot, where it served the neighborhood for years. Eventually, the company decided to close the place and build just a few blocks west. Workers tore the old building down, and the lot filled with trash and graffiti. Although the property occupies less than an acre, its changed appearance affects the whole neighborhood.

No one seems to be jumping to occupy the vacant commercial and residential spaces I passed by on Virginia Avenue south of Meramec Street or South Broadway in Carondelet. Signs of decline—trash, graffiti, and broken glass—appear on block after block. The city's population loss certainly must be a factor. The majority of South Side neighborhoods have lost population since the 1950s, but others have experienced growth, including St. Louis Hills, Soulard, Lafayette Square, and Holly Hills.

The South Side's growing diversity could help reverse the trend. In 1990, 14 percent of the South Side's population consisted of African Americans, and by 2020, that number was 25 percent. Refugees and immigrants have also gravitated to the South Side. Long after the Germans, French, Irish, and Italians found homes on the South Side, refugees from Bosnia established a vibrant community in the Bevo neighborhood. More recently, refugees from Afghanistan and Ukraine have settled in the city, joining sizable populations of Vietnamese, Somalis, Bhutanese, and Iraqis. The refugees and immigrants in St. Louis could make up a small

United Nations. George Sells, director of communications and marketing for the St. Louis Public Schools, said the district educates students from 60 countries. A good number of the students attend schools that teach English as a second language, of which there are 18. You'll find other examples of ethnic richness along the South Grand business district, where myriad international restaurants serve ethnic delights.

South City's endless supply of characters or originals also gives us hope, including people like Jovanka Hammond, owner of Hammonds Books on Cherokee Street Antique Row. Her eclectic used bookstore, connected to a whiskey distillery and brewery, boasts an impressive collection of rare and out-of-print books. Other South Siders have also made their marks as unique characters.

The late Slim and Zella Mae Cox earned a living selling furniture stuffed into a storefront on Chippewa Street. Hailing from Arkansas, they played down-home gospel music for visiting customers. And city patronage worker Mickey McTague wrote material for Bob Hope and Joe Garagiola when he wasn't raising a glass with mayors, aldermen, Senator Thomas Eagleton, Governor Mel Carnahan, and *Post-Dispatch* columnist Bill McClellan.

I've met a bunch of these characters during my time in South City. They've all influenced these parts in their own unique ways. Not convinced? Join me on my jaunt, and I'll show you.

The Mud House on Cherokee.
Courtesy Jim Merkel

St. Francis de Sales Oratory

WALKING IN THE FOOTSTEPS OF ULYSSES GRANT

Gravois Avenue to Chippewa Street

St. Louisans who love history speak with pride of the day in February 1764 when a 14-year-old named René Auguste Chouteau led a group of 30 to where the grounds of the Gateway Arch currently stand. Chouteau supervised the men as they started to build a fur-trading post for Pierre Laclède Liguest. Later, Chouteau drew a map of the original village that mostly showed a series of residential streets and a road heading southwest. This thoroughfare stops at the map's end, but it's easy to imagine Chouteau wanting the road to extend further west. Until his death in 1829, Chouteau helped lead the village that would eventually become a major American city.

The desire to connect St. Louis to those outside its borders, including to the southwest, deepened. As early as 1804, records mentioned a road that could fit the bill. Natives, inspired by a nearby creek full of gravel, chose a word for the name that locals would forever butcher: Gravois, from two French words meaning "gravely creek." In 1818, Chouteau joined with leaders of St.

Louis and the area beyond in signing a petition to set part of the road's path into what is now St. Louis County. The new Gravois Road became the southern boundary of land owned by one of the signers of the petition, Thomas Hunt. Hunt would sell the land to Frederick F. Dent. In time, Gravois became a state road, complete and covered with a macadam pavement. Dent's land took on the name White Haven, and from 1854 to 1859, his son-in-law Ulysses S. Grant farmed the land before later becoming president. Often, Grant brought farming goods and firewood into St. Louis to sell. He likely took Gravois Road into St. Louis, because what else would he have used? Many used Gravois for travel and still do.

The road became a main street at different stretches for South City and communities like Affton, Crestwood, Sunset Hills, and Fenton. In the 1960s, Interstate I-44 became the preferred route for the motorists who wanted to save time on the commute home. In many cases, though, Gravois still is the best way on the South Side to get to Schnucks, Walgreens, a mechanic, a corner bar, or the home of a friend.

On January 16, 2021, I started a hike of Gravois where Tucker Boulevard merges with 12th Street and becomes Gravois Avenue. My goal was to follow Grant's likely path home from work to Chippewa Street, which accounts for about 2.9 miles. So began my yearlong zigzag, 45-mile-long walk through South City.

The temperature was 36 degrees, not too frigid for January 16 but cold for a three-mile trek. Wearing three sweaters beneath a heavy jacket should keep away some of the cold, I thought. I hoped. I started off under a sign that informs those headed southwest they're on Gravois. Above are the overpasses for Interstates 44 and 55. Ahead, an ocean of concrete and asphalt surrounds vacant buildings and commercial structures, with a sprinkling of brick apartments and churches. I walked toward Russell Boulevard, crossed Gravois, and arrived next to a Jack in the Box. Further

ST. MICHAEL THE ARCHANGEL RUSSIAN ORTHODOX CHURCH.

A. 19 ✝ 28 D.

РУССКАЯ ПРАВОСЛАВНАЯ СВ. АРХИСТРАТИГА МИХАИЛА ЦЕРКОВЬ.

southwest is the A-1 Wok Takeout and Delivery followed by St. Michael the Archangel Orthodox Church. According to the church's website, St. Michael's has been a part of the St. Louis community since 1909. The website says parishioners spent two decades raising money to build the Byzantine-style temple before they finished and dedicated it in 1929. At that time, their temple faced part of Highway 66.

Across Gravois from St. Michael the Archangel and a bit to the right is a monstrous, empty building that brewed beer more than a century ago. That building, at Shenandoah Avenue and Lemp Street, turned out beer for the Griesedieck Brothers Brewery before and after prohibition. From 1957 to 1977, it brewed Falstaff, a favorite local brand. Nearby, the Falstaff Corporation touted itself with the Falstaff Museum of Brewing in the Tudor-style Falstaff Inn, but the glory faded when the company went bust. The brewery and the inn stand empty along with many other vacant buildings between Tucker and Grand Boulevard.

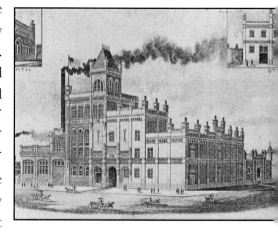

Consumers Brewing Company, Southwest corner of Shenandoah and Lemp Avenues. Courtesy Missouri Historical Society, St. Louis

When buildings went vacant, so did nearby restaurants, with one exception. Hodak's, a local icon, has served fried chicken at 2100

Gravois since 1962. At one time, Hodak's was one of four fried-chicken restaurants along Gravois. They included Medich's, Lemmon's, and Mary's Fine Foods. Lemmon's, to the west, is open but offers Balkan fare. Another food option on Gravois near Hodak's that looks attractive is Egg, a breakfast and lunch place housed in the restored Polar Wave Ice & Fuel Building. Few others stand out.

The corner of Jefferson Avenue and Gravois stands out but not in a good way. At the southeast corner, Bank of America occupies a beaux-arts building, built in 1925 as the Jefferson-Gravois Bank and later renovated in 1956. Also at the corner are a chain chicken place, a tattoo shop, a convenience store, and two payday loan outfits. Old photos show lovely buildings at that corner in their original glory, but those businesses and the ambience they imparted are long gone.

Jefferson-Gravois Bank in 1925.
Courtesy Missouri Historical Society, St. Louis

Kutis Funeral Home with St. Francis de Sales Oratory in the distance

A few churches line the street heading west, but one towers over all others. With a 300-foot steeple, St. Francis de Sales Catholic Church is a soaring architectural gem and a landmark. Dedicated in 1908, the church replaced another that was demolished by the Great Cyclone of 1896. It surpassed anything that seven German immigrant dairymen could have imagined when they bought a tract at Gravois and Ohio Avenue for a new parish in 1867. Designed to match a Gothic church in Germany, the building contains a 50-foot-tall altar and a 130-foot-long aisle. The church interior is filled with Gothic arches and stained-glass windows.

Known as the Cathedral of South St. Louis, the church looked magnificent when 7,000 to 9,000 families, mostly German-American, attended Mass there. Its glory dimmed when attendance dropped to 50 or 60 individuals and forced the parish to close in 2005. But a new priestly order, Christ the King Sovereign Priest, came along and now administers the traditional Latin Mass there. Today, 800 to 1,000 people from all over the metro area attend one of two Sunday Masses of St. Francis de Sales Oratory. Current numbers would be enough to support the upkeep of any modern church building but not one as old as St. Francis de Sales. Members struggle to pay the bills, but hopefully the Archdiocese of St. Louis sees the value of maintaining the place. The magnificence of the building and its spire redeem the rough edges of Gravois east of Grand Boulevard with a grandeur seen in few South City neighborhoods.

One of the best places to view the church is uphill to the west, in the parking lot of the Kutis Funeral Home. At its peak in the early 1970s, the home held around 1,200 to 1,300 funerals a year. Now, because of Kutis locations in Affton and South County, the city home holds only about 250. What it lacks in business it makes up for in historical character. Designed by the architectural firm Froese, Maack, and Becker and built in 1931, the building features a sloping tile roof and beige brick on the outside. Stunning plasterwork adorns the inside, which includes two living quarters upstairs. Tom Kutis III, whose son and grandson help operate the business, remembers when his grandparents lived there. His aunt moved into one of the units after she married. Tom III didn't get a chance to live there, but he remembers many details from the past, including the fact that his family didn't originally have carpet laid. Too many mourners smoked, and dropped cigarettes would have left burn marks.

Just west of Kutis stand nondescript commercial buildings, some empty and some occupied. I noticed a message scrawled in marker on plywood that covers a window: "How can Satan cast out Satan? And if a kingdom is divided against itself, the kingdom cannot stand, and if a house is divided against itself, it cannot stand." I pondered the message as I came upon an abundance of used car lots. From St. Francis de Sales west to Compton Avenue—a distance of seven-tenths of a mile—nine different dealers hawk their vehicles, with many promoting their financing.

The road slopes down after the smorgasbord of cars. It provided some relief as I scanned the campus of Roosevelt High School from the opposite side of the street. The school opened in January 1925 after McKinley and Cleveland High Schools filled up. Roosevelt's teams have always been the Roughriders, named after the famous cavalry unit led by Theodore Roosevelt during the Spanish–American War. The school might have picked "ghosts" as

Roosevelt High School

the nickname because the old Picker Cemetery once occupied the site. The bodies, which were removed before construction began, ended up at the city morgue. Some had to be identified, including a corpse dressed smartly in the uniform of a Civil War captain. The coroner told a reporter that he would request burial at the Jefferson Barracks National Cemetery. Here's hoping the soldier found peace at Jefferson Barracks.

Cherokee Street appears just west of Roosevelt. The Mexican and antique shops on the artery beckoned, but I decided to save that for another day. I started to get hungry after passing the Caribbean Delight Jamaican restaurant. Gravois plays host to a number of international eateries, including Chinese, Somalian, Arab, and Vietnamese, among others. They might lack the polish of ethnic restaurants in the South Grand international district, but they still show how much various nationalities influence the city. During my time as a reporter for the old *South Side Journal*, an editor told me to track down the St. Paul sandwich, a delicacy that emerged decades ago at local Chinese restaurants. The concoction consists of an egg foo young patty (fried), iceberg lettuce, sliced tomatoes, dill pickles, and mayonnaise served on white bread. My investigation led to the Kim Van Chinese Restaurant, where I ordered one. It

South Side National Bank in 1929.
Courtesy Missouri Historical Society, St. Louis

wasn't for me, but I could appreciate the appeal.

Approaching Grand Boulevard, I took notice of a three-story building. It originally housed the Farmers & Merchants Trust Co., but Patricia's: Where Fun and Fantasy Meet now occupies the storefront. I didn't investigate further. I walked across Grand and looked up at the 10-story building that South Side National Bank once owned. Locals from all walks of life attended the building's dedication in 1929. Its art deco design reflected 1920s grandeur. To thwart prospective robbers, the company put its banking operation on the second floor, which customers could reach by grand staircase or elevator. The next year should have promised great things for the new bank, but the Depression hit and forced South Side National to close and reorganize. A bank remained in the building until the 1990s, when protests by neighborhood groups halted plans to demolish the building and replace it with a Walgreens and a smaller bank building. The building stayed and was eventually converted to condominiums. Residents can cook from a barbecue pit on the roof and feast on a view of the surrounding neighborhoods. If not for the protests, the southwest corner of Grand and Gravois might look more like Jefferson and Gravois.

After reaching the bank, I turned back to the east side of Grand and hopped on an eastbound bus. It took me back to my car, where I had started the hike. On another day, I'd finish my walk to Chippewa Street. The upcoming stretch of Gravois can hardly be called spectacular. Still, Ulysses Grant would see the present-day highway as an acceptable route for transporting farm goods and firewood to market.

Donut Drive-In
Courtesy Jim Merkel

A RIDE ON ROUTE 66

Chippewa Street from Gravois Avenue to Jamieson Avenue

As I started walking along Chippewa Street just west of Gravois, I spotted an abandoned shopping cart from Aldi in an empty used car lot. That sight did not surprise me, since abandoned items, including assorted trash, appear all over this stretch of Chippewa. Chippewa is one of several east-west streets in South City that extend from near the Mississippi River all the way to the city's western boundary. Most of those streets stay east of Grand Boulevard but not Chippewa. As part of Route 66, it once served as the main pathway for travelers headed from Chicago to Los Angeles.

I encountered the lonely shopping cart near the railroad viaduct, a familiar site for employees who worked at the nearby building that produced the old *Suburban Journals* for South St. Louis and South St. Louis County. During my tenure, I would sometimes walk to the highest point of the viaduct and look back at the building. Inside, we produced news stories and features about the surrounding neighborhoods and beyond. From 1994 to 2009, I sat in a chair at the same spot in the same cubicle in the newsroom. The company paid just enough for us to drive 10-year-old cars. Nonetheless, we had a sense of one-for-all, all-for-one and believed our tasks were important. Some of my coworkers were unusual, like one guy who was constantly angry. One morning, he arrived late for a discussion about a front-page article in that morning's *Post-Dispatch* that he normally covered. When he demanded to see the story in his usual loud voice, I picked up the *PD* edition with the story and shoved it close to his face. "Here it is," I said. Pow! I felt the impact on the left side of my face. The boss fired him on the spot. He also put a note in my file saying I had baited the belligerent reporter. The next week, my coworkers feted me with fried chicken at Hodak's. The meal was nice, but I wish the confrontation hadn't happened. If he reads this, I wish him well.

I appreciated my coworkers in general, because we were proud of covering the little things, like neighborhood meetings in South City and city-council meetings at small municipalities in South County. No other newspapers put the closing of a Catholic grade school at the top of page one. I talked to local leaders that I never would have met otherwise. It was the best 15 years of my career.

In May 2009, we learned the company was closing the building and shipping us to an office in West County. The day I left, I moved the last of my personal items out of a partially-disassembled office to my car. Five minutes later, I returned to find everything gone, including my cubicle. I transferred to the Illinois office the next year. My job was never the same. The company laid most of us off in 2013, including me. After that, I took early retirement and got by mostly on part-time writing jobs. The way I see it, my career really ended the day we moved out of the big gray building by the viaduct.

I turned away from the building I remember so well and walked over railroad tracks.

I stopped for the day at Morgan Ford Road and resumed my journey west in 24-degree weather the next day. Within a matter of blocks, I came upon the former site of the shopping jewel of the South Side at the corner of Chippewa and Kingshighway. Starting in 1951, Southtown Famous-Barr outclassed any merchandiser in South City. In her book *Famous-Barr: St. Louis Shopping at its Finest*, Edna Campos Gravenhorst provided a long list of go-beyond amenities sold at the four-floor department store. Shoppers could pay utility bills, dine at the Mississippi Room, buy furniture and every appliance imaginable, get their picture taken, and have their jewelry fixed. The store not only offered merchandise, it also lent strollers to customers with babies and staffed a first-aid center. Access was also made easy with a parking lot adjacent to the building and another directly across Chippewa. The latter funneled customers into the store via an underground tunnel.

People mourned when Southtown Famous closed in 1992. During the demolition, I swiped a brick as a souvenir, but I don't know where it is anymore. The store was eventually replaced by a strip center with useful stuff like office supplies, fancy coffee, eateries, and pet food, but the customer experience will never match shopping at Southtown Famous.

A century ago, Chippewa ended at Kingshighway Boulevard, but the city decided in the early 1920s to extend Chippewa to Watson, mostly through fields, truck farms, and clay mines. The extension would provide a link to the proposed Ozark Trail. In 1932, the state widened Chippewa and Watson from Kingshighway into St. Louis County. This filled the city's last undeveloped section and led to a boom in home construction.

As I followed the trail west, I noticed a change in building style. West of Brannon are neat brick homes. A left turn on Macklind would have taken me into the Southampton neighborhood. Known for brick arts and crafts homes built mostly in the 1930s, Southampton features streets with English-sounding names like Murdoch, Devonshire, not to mention Hampton, the north-south thoroughfare for southwest St. Louis. Macklind Avenue hosts a small but healthy business district with merchants who sell everything from high-class ice cream

Clementine's Ice Cream on Macklind

to coffee to pizza. The neighborhood's annual fall festival occurs on the last Saturday in September. Macklind from Devonshire to Nottingham closes down and becomes a center for live music, food and drink vendors, and a kid zone complete with a bounce house.

Modern, multifamily brick apartment buildings dominate Chippewa west of Macklind. Then comes the Williamsburg Colonial-style Hampton Village Shopping Center, which opened in 1939 at the southeast corner of Chippewa and Hampton. Developer Harry Brinkop attracted early tenants like Bettendorf's market, S. S. Kresge, and J. C. Penney, which operated there for 70 years until it closed in 2017.

The cold finally got to me at the corner of Hampton at Chippewa. I realized I was too cold to walk another mile to my ending point—Jamieson Avenue—but where could I stop? I passed Target on the left and worried nothing else would be open because of COVID-19 restrictions. Had it been warmer, Ron Elz could have joined my walk. Ron, a local historian and radio personality who also goes by the name Johnny Rabbitt, grew up in the neighborhood north of Chippewa and now lives in St. Louis Hills. As a kid, he would watch the traffic on Chippewa

and would notice cars with state license plates and big trucks with words like "Campbell's 66 Express" painted on the side. Ron could have directed me to the nearest restaurant that didn't offer fast food. The answer to my prayers came in the form of an IHOP, known formally as the International House of Pancakes. I decided to finish my route on another day and grabbed something to eat. After I called my wife and asked her to pick me up, I let my bones warm while scarfing down a BLT. Nothing better.

In the following days, temperatures plummeted, but when the mercury rose to 14 degrees, I restarted my route at the IHOP wearing three sweaters, a hat, scarf, and gloves. I was ready for action. The first notable site was the Grecian columns of Hoffmeister Mortuary. The Georgian colonial-style funeral home looked stately in the winter snow, just as I'm sure it did when it opened in 1938. The building first housed the Great Western Livery Stable, opened by a German immigrant named Christian Hoffmeister in 1858. When townspeople appealed to him to provide hearses and carriages for funeral processions, Hoffmeister found himself in the funeral business. The company stayed in the family until it was sold to a national group of mortuaries

Hoffmeister Funeral Home

in 1986. Today, Hoffmeister is part of another national company, Dignity Memorial.

The place looked quiet, but a little further down Chippewa and across the street is a place that's seldom quiet, especially in the morning. The Donut Drive-In has been a Route 66 icon in St. Louis since it opened in the early 1950s. You can smell, see, and taste what makes their donuts special when you enter the tiny shop at 6525 Chippewa Street. Donut Drive-In has maintained its original character with the help of the National Park Service and the Missouri 66 Association's Neon Heritage Preservation Committee. Both parties kicked in to restore the signage, which includes a gorgeous, retro, neon sign that beckons to motorists at night.

Other eateries long provided sustenance on this stretch of Chippewa, though many are now gone. At the southwest corner of Lansdowne Avenue and Chippewa, teenagers used to hang out and devour stringy fries and shakes at an old Steak 'n Shake that lasted more than 50 years until a grease fire destroyed the joint. A Starbucks now stands in its place. At about 3:30 p.m. several months after my walk along Chippewa, I entered that Starbucks and found it filled with girls wearing school uniforms. One of them mentioned that they were from St. Gabriel the Archangel School a few blocks away in St. Louis Hills. These early teens were dabbling in the grown-up art of drinking coffee.

Chippewa also lost Garavelli's, a busy, cafeteria-style restaurant that served comfort food: meat loaf, turkey with dressing, stewed tomatoes, and other favorites of grandmas 60 years ago. Changing tastes brought Garavelli's to an end in 2013, but longtime customers were nonetheless saddened. A credit union has replaced it.

A different kind of eatery—one that also sells groceries—faces Donovan Avenue, just south of Chippewa. LeGrand's Market & Catering prospers today, just as an earlier mom-and-pop grocery did in the same space. William Binder built the original store in the mid-1930s. Cornfields filled the west, but Binder wanted a business near Cyrus Willmore's new St. Louis Hills development. Binder ran the store until the mid-1950s, when his son William Binder Jr. took over. In 1987, Binder Jr. sold the store to employee Jim LeGrand, who said he knew the business, the neighborhood, and the potential. LeGrand kept the Tom Boy sign out front but made changes inside. When he started selling sandwiches at the meat counter, customers flocked. The sandwiches were so popular, he removed half or more of the groceries and replaced them with indoor seating, adding outdoor seating as well. On fair-weather days at LeGrand's, you'll find businesspeople, families, and retirees socializing over lunch. You might also catch pre-teens from the neighborhood on their first unattended outing with friends. Meeting up at LeGrand's has become a rite of passage for new generations. People line up for lunchtime favorites like the Great Bambino or the Hoagie Berra just as often as they line up for their favorite concrete at Ted Drewes.

Which was where I was heading that day despite the cold. The Ted Drewes Frozen Custard stand is a

sight to behold. The stand opened in 1941 with faux wooden icicles hanging down from the façade, less than 20 yards after Chippewa continued as Watson Road. When I got there, I observed one woman waiting for her order at one of the service windows. If it seems strange that a woman would wait outside for a frozen treat to eat in the biting cold, you haven't had a Ted Drewes concrete.

Had it been a broiling night in July or August, hundreds might have shown up for a cool Southern Delight, a Dottie, or, my personal favorite, the hot fudge concrete. The typical transaction takes just minutes, but lines on a busy night might keep you for a while. It doesn't please Travis Dillon when that happens. He owns the business with his wife, Christy. They'd rather keep the customers happy, not just the ones at this location (which also sells Christmas trees in the winter), but also the ones who patronize his custard stand at 4224 S. Grand Blvd. Christy is the daughter of Ted Drewes Jr., who's famous for holding one of the company's products in commercials and announcing, "It really is good, guys. . . and gals." All three of Travis and Christy's kids worked at Ted Drewes, and their two sons have made it a career. Putting kids and grandkids to work for eager customers has been the family's way since Ted Sr. started his very first frozen custard stand in Florida, circa 1929.

I didn't stop for ice cream that day, because the cold was getting to me, specifically to my feet. I continued toward Jamieson, where Catholic Supply of Greater St. Louis anchors the northeast corner. Catholic Supply replaced a furniture store in 2000. Not satisfied with a standard ribbon-cutting, the owner tapped Archbishop Justin Rigali to bless the place at its grand opening.

I considered stopping in, but Lorraine waited at the corner. As I hopped into my wife's car, I yearned for July and the taste of a hot fudge concrete.

St. Louis Hills
Courtesy Don Korte

I FOLLOW A REAL ESTATE GENIUS

St. Louis Hills

Drivers on Jamieson Avenue may not know it, but whenever they utter the street's name, they honor a Scottish family known for their clay mines. Today, the street provides a route to a neighborhood that resembles St. Louis County as much as it does the city. St. Louis Hills was the perfect combination of urban and suburban housing. Cyrus Crane Willmore had a dream: provide city dwellers of all income levels with the finest in country living, with solid brick houses, duplexes, and apartments. The Great Depression threatened to scuttle the dream just as work started, but Willmore didn't let that stop him. He insisted on high standards of workmanship the whole way, and the 700-acre St. Louis Hills development finally came to fruition decades later.

I began my journey through "the Hills" at the southeast corner of Jamieson and Chippewa street, shortly before 2 p.m., July 17. I walked south by the stately Trinity Assembly of God before making a left on Devonshire Avenue. The adjacent street, Murdoch Avenue, would have taken me through the set of blocks that become Candy Cane Lane in late November and most of December every year. Two Christmases earlier, I watched cars and buses crawl down the line, with the eyes inside of each transfixed on the dense array of Christmas lights and fixtures. Candy Cane Lane has become a holiday institution in the neighborhood, but others have cropped up as well. They include Snow Flake Street, Angel Avenue, and Llama Lane (with its Santa mailbox). Their displays help celebrate the season, along with events like the Christmas Tree Lighting in Francis Park, the Santa Parade, and the neighborhood holiday party.

Donovan Avenue marks the end of Candy Cane Lane. Development surrounds that intersection today, but in 1931,

Willmore Development Office in St. Louis Hills, 1928. Courtesy Missouri Historical Society, St. Louis

it was part of a field with one lonely building nearby: the offices of the Cyrus Crane Willmore Organization. In the Roaring Twenties, Willmore earned a reputation for developing major home projects in the area, each possessing class seen in few other developments. He called them University Park, University Hills, Kingshighway Hills, Webster Hills, and Wellston Hills. Willmore loved the word Hills; it suggested his subdivisions stood on high ground. At the start of the 1930s, he made the word "Hills" part of his biggest project yet: St. Louis Hills. The street system wasn't finished before the construction of St. Louis Hills began, but the neighborhood was surrounded by key arteries like Chippewa Street, Hampton Avenue, Gravois Avenue, and River des Peres.

St. Louis Hills residents today live in homes with a variety of styles that range from art deco to Colonial to Tudor to ranch. Houses contain generous amounts of cast concrete, aluminum, stonework, and glass blocks. Stately turrets jut from a few of the neighborhood's houses, and on others, stone surrounds the top of arched wooden doors, giving some of the dwellings a gingerbread look. For renters, there are whole city blocks full of four-family, two-story apartment buildings with a single main entrance. Like the houses, many have their own personality and character, yet all possess elegance and beauty. While he was developing the neighborhood, Willmore approved all designs of the homes and apartments. All were brick, topped with roofs of slate or tile. Trees and shrubs were plentiful, and rose bushes lined the streets. New residents in the area were shown a warm welcome, receiving a bouquet of roses the day they moved in.

Walking past the homes on Donovan took me to Nottingham Avenue and the edge of Francis Park. A church faces each corner of the park: Thomas the Apostle Orthodox Church (NW), Ascension Lutheran Church (SW), Hope United Church of Christ (SE), and finally St. Gabriel (NE), a white stone Gothic structure with a steeple that rises twelve stories. Before St. Gabe's opened in 1951, priests celebrated Masses in the basement of a school completed in 1935 on Tamm near Nottingham. The school remains vibrant to this day.

The charm of St. Louis Hills is, and was, undeniable. The neighborhood attracted notable residents like Red Schoendienst, Joe Garagiola, and Stan

St. Gabriel the
Archangel Church

Musial. Lifelong St. Louis Hills resident Paul Ritter recalled that Musial's wife kept to herself. But if Musial was home, he'd invite kids in and sign autographs.

St. Louis Hills has hosted other notables, among them orthodontist Howard C. Ohlendorf, who ran twice for Congress as a Republican and lost both times. After that, he quipped that the voters had given him an overwhelming mandate to stay home. He was more successful in saving the Forest Park Highlands carousel after its surroundings burned in 1963. He donated the carousel to St. Louis County's Sylvan Springs Park, restored it 15 years later, and then gave it to the County's Faust Park. He also donated the fountains for the lakes at Tilles and Queeny Parks in the County and for Carondelet Park in south St. Louis.

While walking in Francis Park, I passed couples walking dogs and women jogging in bright outfits. Past Delor and just before Walsh Street, I spied a sidewalk leading to the center of Francis Park and headed for it. The path leads downhill to a seven-foot-tall bronze statue of David Rowland Francis standing boldly in the middle of the park. With a supersized top hat, mustache, and three-piece suit, this rendering depicts a leader of consequence. Francis was the mayor of St. Louis, governor of Missouri, Secretary of the Interior for President Grover Cleveland, and the president and chief pitchman of the St. Louis World's Fair. To boot, he served a harrowing term as ambassador to Russia during the Bolshevik revolution.

The park bears Francis's name because he donated the land to the city in 1916. Looking out from the pedestal, I saw ballfields and tennis courts in addition to handball, racquetball, and pickleball courts. It's a sports lover's playground, all in close range to an actual playground. A long, narrow lily pond allows for more leisurely recreation. Perfect for a stroll, the lily pond also anchors both an art fair and a beer festival.

On the south side of the park adjacent to the tennis courts, craft brewer Rockwell Brewing Co. opened a beer garden in a stone building once used for park maintenance operations. Rockwell serves beer and tavern-style pizza, which park visitors often enjoy during events like the Tour de Francis Park cycling event or the Run for the Hills 5K race. Not all events take place in the park. A popular house tour showcases Willmore's masterworks while raising money for the St. Louis Hills Neighborhood Association.

The president of that group is Nancy Vordtriede, who has lived in the Hills since she was born in 1962. She remembers her dad saying that the lower part of Highfield toward St. Raphael the Archangel Church was once swamp land. She loved riding her bike in Francis Park, especially along the lily pond. Her dad served on the board of the neighborhood association and helped make sure I-44 steered clear of St. Louis Hills.

The neighborhood has always looked out for itself and has enjoyed highlighting its own. In 1934, Willmore started a lush monthly magazine that did more than puff his houses. The *News of St. Louis Hills* featured photos of the neighborhood's best gardens, gushed about the moving picture theater at the home of L. A. Benson at 6557 Itaska Street, and offered housekeeping tips for new brides. A page of odds and ends announced that the Shell Oil Company had promoted Mr. Purdon C. Thomas of 6227 Loran to division manager.

Pride remains a hallmark of St. Louis Hills residents. As I left the park and headed south on Donovan, I saw an assortment of richly colored flags—American, Cardinals, and even a Union Jack—hanging from the façades of houses. They added pageantry to the scene. After I continued across Eichelberger, the homes took on a post-war suburban look—one-story, ranch style, still brick but a lighter color that leaned toward yellow. Some streets in this area south of Eichelberger, which Willmore branded St. Louis Hills Estates, with many brick ranch homes.

Rockwell Brewing Co.
on the south side of
Francis Park

Drinks & Concessions

Continuing south, I eventually reached Highfield Road and St. Raphael Church, a Colonial-style structure built in 1950. Its red brick, white columns, and narrow white spire—characteristic of many Protestant churches in the region—make St. Raphael's stand out from other Catholic churches in the city. Farther south of the church on Jamieson sits a sprawling park on land donated mostly by Willmore himself. Willmore Park borders the eastern bank of the River des Peres and features rolling hills and a bike trail that surround two lakes. Chris Saracino, who owns and oversees Chris' Pancake House, grew up in St. Louis Hills and loved fishing those lakes. He also remembers ice skating on them in the winter and playing softball on the ballfields at each end of the park.

These days, disc golf has taken over as the preferred warm-weather sport at Willmore. 18 baskets appear at different spots spread throughout the park. Casual and serious players flock to the ample, hilly course, either to play informally or to participate in tournaments.

St. Raphael Catholic Church

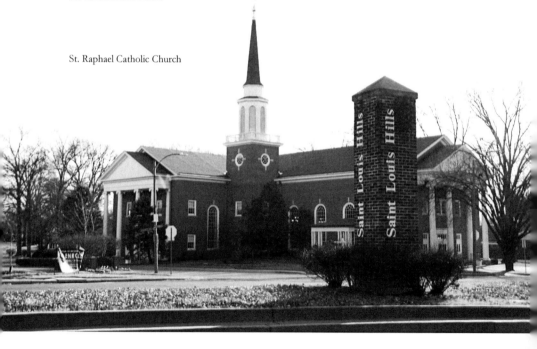

As I reached the south end of the park, which marked the end of his magnificent neighborhood, I thought of Willmore's own end. He died in 1949 of heart disease at the age of 59. Three years later, the *News of St. Louis Hills* published its last edition. It noted that around 10,000 people now lived in the neighborhood. That, the magazine said, was a monument to Cyrus Crane Willmore.

North Lake in Willmore Park

Bevo Mill

ROWS OF GRAVES AND A WINDMILL

Gravois Avenue and Hampton Avenue to Chippewa Street and Morgan Ford Road

T he sun hung large, bright, and low in the morning haze of August 4 as I started on Gravois heading east from Germania. The view made me glad I had awakened before dawn for this particular walk. At 6:45, before I left the house, I sat dazed and groggy waiting for Larry, my walking partner for the day. When he arrived, I hopped into his car, and he told me that our outing would complement his exercise regimen. At 71, he rode his bike three mornings a week and lifted weights the other three.

Larry exercises not only to maintain his strength but to slow the progression of his Parkinson's disease. The first signs of it appeared seven years ago, but I rarely see his hands shaking. Regardless, I knew he wouldn't struggle with the two-and-a-half-mile route planned for the day.

You can call Larry a pastor or an elder at my church, but his real title should be "helper." His stewardship has affected us deeply. Larry's the one who arranges the memorial services for members without families, delivers meals to the hungry, and makes sure everyone is heard at our midweek church meetings. And he joins the likes of yours truly for 7 a.m. walks.

At 7:03, we walked past the buses in the Hampton-Gravois Transit Center, where I activated my pedometer app and continued east with Larry through the Schnucks and McDonald's parking lots. We passed Gatewood Gardens Cemetery, which has land on both sides of Gravois. The city took control of the cemetery in the mid-1990s after the owner, who kept lousy records of the interred and their gravesites, failed to pay property taxes. After seizing ownership, the city held an auction for a buyer but nobody bid, so the city's Land Reutilization Authority remains in the graveyard business to this day.

After passing the cemetery, we saw a St. Louis institution on our left. Parents have been buying kids their first bikes at South Side Cyclery ever since Velmo Chappuis started the store on Meramec Street in 1933. Today, Tim Kakouris ("TK"), a former pro BMX racer, and his wife, Deanna, now own the place. When

I visited on a different day, Deanna mentioned that sales have jumped since the start of the pandemic. Many Bosnians in the neighborhood ride bikes, and so do younger people who've moved into the city. Deanna loves riding around the area and told me that when she bikes, she sees things she wouldn't notice otherwise.

One of those things might be the South St. Louis American Legion Memorial Post 37, which sits back from Gravois on Dahlia Avenue. If you look closely, you'll see a weapon that once had the power to take out a house as far away as South County. The 75 MM Light Field Gun, with a barrel almost three inches in diameter, sits idle and harmless but was once deadly. One round could obliterate a house, and a few dozen more could take out a neighborhood. The French first built the weapon in 1897, and it saw extensive use during World War I. The particular model—number 228—was manufactured in 1919 and acquired by Post 37 in the 1960s. Placed into storage after Vietnam War protesters targeted it, the cannon went back on display in 2003 for new generations to view, provided they observe the "keep off" sign.

East of the legion post, two very narrow parks run along Christy Boulevard near its intersection with Gravois. Owners who live in houses that face both parks might feel like they live on the world's biggest lawn. Christy Boulevard separates Christy Park north of Gravois from Joseph R. Leisure Park south of Gravois. The former is named after William Tandy Christy, founder of the Laclede-Christy Fire Brick Company, and the latter after a city employee who worked 45 years in jobs that included director of parks, recreation, and forestry. Titles for city parks go to all kinds of people but especially for minor politicians and patronage officials.

Past Christy Boulevard, we encountered one of the few remaining examples of turnvereins, or gymnastics societies that early German immigrants used to develop sound minds and bodies. The facility for the Concordia Gymnastic Society comprises two gymnasiums, an outdoor pool, and a sand volleyball court. One member, George Eyser, took gold in the 1904 St. Louis Olympics for horse vault, parallel bars, and rope climbing. He also won two silver medals and one bronze medal, and he did it all with a wooden left leg.

East of Christy Park, the names on the windows are harder to spell. We're in the Bevo Mill area, which became a Bosnian refugee community in the mid-1990s. Their hard work and cultural contributions have blessed the whole region but especially the struggling Bevo Mill. The neighborhood now is packed with Bosnian restaurants, bars, grocery stores, and coffee shops, including Café Milano. The building that now houses the Café Milano once hosted Gravois Bootery, one of those places with cubby holes filled with shoeboxes on every part of the wall. The

smell of leather was ever present, and salespeople would measure your feet and bring out shoes till you found the right fit. I felt like a king when my stepmother bought me a pair at the Gravois Bootery in the late 1970s.

In 1960, the blocks near the bootery offered the same purpose as a shopping center. Businesses nearby included Joe's Tailor Shop, A&P Food Store, and Top Flight Sandwich Shop. Most of the shops left, partly because the neighborhood declined and partly because people didn't want to shop for jewelry or clothes on a gritty stretch of Gravois. Today,

bars, restaurants, specialty
shops, and other oddities fill
many of the storefronts.

Across the street from
Café Milano are two
businesses that typify the new
Bevo: Heavy Anchor Bar
& Venue and the adjoining
Arkadin Cinema & Bar.
The Heavy Anchor offers
concerts, comedy shows, and
other events. Owner Jodie Timbrook believes that the area is turning
into an entertainment and business district with a young audience.
At Arkadin Cinema & Bar, named for a character in an Orson Welles
film, owners Keith Watson and Sarah Baraba intended to show
classic flicks to small crowds, but COVID-19 scotched their plans.
So the Heavy Anchor offered to let Arkadin project their movies in
a lot behind the bar. Since then, Watson and Baraba have renovated
and opened a microcinema on Gravois. Heavy Anchor attracted
more customers, and the cinema was able to stay in business. On a
perfect evening in September, I sat under the stars and watched The
Freshman, a Harold Lloyd silent movie about a new college student's
bumbling efforts to find popularity, football glory, and love.

After taking in the highlights on Gravois, we veered toward
Morgan Ford Road, which some argue is really Morganford. City
maps have shown it both ways through the years, and even signs
have spelled it differently. We do know the road once led to a ford
on the River des Peres operated by a man named Morgan.

I hoped Stuart Baker, records retention supervisor for the city
comptroller's office, could help settle the debate. He keeps track of
really old ordinances, from 1851 to 1949. He has concluded, based
on the earliest ordinance that mentions the road, that the most likely

spelling was originally Morgan Ford. That one designated a portion of the road south of Arsenal as Morgan Ford. Baker did not find any other naming ordinance about the road, but it makes sense that other naming ordinances would have the same spelling. Lacking anything else, I'm sticking with two words.

Together, Morgan Ford and Gravois form an "X." On the east side of that "X" is the Miniature Museum of Greater St. Louis. In the museum, an exhibit of teensy people prepare for a banquet at tiny tables set with itty-bitty china. In another scene, a pianist sits at a micro grand piano. In yet another, a Lilliputian-sized bathroom is complete with a sink, bathtub, and toilet.

Bevo Mill in the 1930s.
Courtesy Missouri Historical Society, St. Louis

Looming outside of the museum, just across the street, is a local landmark that's not so miniature. In fact, it's gargantuan. The Bevo Mill stands on a wedge at Gravois and Morgan Ford. Many say that Anheuser-Busch beer baron August Busch Sr. built the massive windmill as a midpoint between his family home at Grant's Farm and the Anheuser-Busch Brewery on Arsenal Street. One can imagine the older Busch stopping by the Bevo for a Budweiser on his way home from the brewery, but Busch went public with a more compelling reason for building the Mill: to fight prohibition. He told a reporter for the *Post-Dispatch* in November 1916 that the way to stop alcohol abuse was to ban all bars that encouraged overuse. He favored establishing the German saloon system, where saloons only sell beer, light wines, and temperance drinks, and patrons couldn't buy drinks for each other. Busch claimed that when bar patrons took turns buying rounds, each person might end up consuming 20 to 30 drinks.

To demonstrate this saloon system, he planned to spend $125,000 in 1917 to build Bevo Mill. At the base of the building, he incorporated colored stones that he'd gathered with his own hands at Grant's Farm. All drinks were served at tables. He named one of the options Bevo, a near-beer with less than a quarter percent of alcohol.

The Bevo Mill failed in its mission to stop Prohibition, but it did succeed as a restaurant, run by different operators through the years. Anheuser-Busch retained ownership of the building until bequeathing it to the city in 2009. Soon after, the restaurant closed, and the mill remained dormant until Carol and Pat Schuchard bought and restored the place. "Das Bevo" now offers Sunday brunch, wedding receptions, and other special events, along with occasional band performances in its charming biergarten.

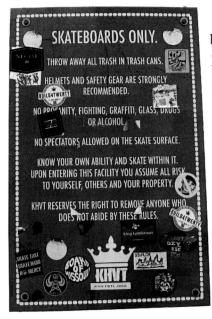

SKATEBOARDS ONLY.

THROW AWAY ALL TRASH IN TRASH CANS.

HELMETS AND SAFETY GEAR ARE STRONGLY RECOMMENDED.

NO PROFANITY, FIGHTING, GRAFFITI, GLASS, DRUGS OR ALCOHOL.

NO SPECTATORS ALLOWED ON THE SKATE SURFACE.

KNOW YOUR OWN ABILITY AND SKATE WITHIN IT. UPON ENTERING THIS FACILITY YOU ASSUME ALL RISK TO YOURSELF, OTHERS AND YOUR PROPERTY.

KHVT RESERVES THE RIGHT TO REMOVE ANYONE WHO DOES NOT ABIDE BY THESE RULES.

After Larry and I admired the biergarten, we continued north on Morgan Ford. At Osceola Street, we passed a small park replete with mini concrete hills and valleys for skaters and skateboarders. The Peter Mathews Memorial Skate Garden, named for a local skater who died in a traffic accident, resulted from the conversion of an old gas station property into a private skatepark. The place stands out as a novelty among mundane brick structures that face the street.

It was the last interesting thing we saw that morning, except maybe a one-story home with the narrowest façade imaginable.

The Peter Mathews Memorial Skate Garden

Soon after, we reached Chippewa. I tapped my toe on the street to mark the conclusion of our journey. I live just blocks away, so we trekked to my car and I took Larry's back to his, parked at the Hampton-Gravois Schnucks. Larry got in his car and headed off to the gym to lift weights.

I returned later to the slim-jim home and I knocked on the door. A man answered, and I asked him how long he had lived there. He said he'd been a tenant for seven or eight years, and before I could get out my follow-up, he closed the door in my face.

THREE SIDES
OF TOWER GROVE SOUTH

Morgan Ford Road to Arsenal Street
to South Grand Boulevard

The sign on the message board at St. John's Lutheran Church reminded me that God isn't like Burger King. You can't have it your way. I smiled at this statement as I started my next jaunt on September 5. Since it was a Sunday, I had just left church and had planned to walk from the corner of Chippewa and Morgan Ford to the corner of Morgan Ford and Arsenal. Then I'd turn right on Arsenal and make another right on South Grand before finishing up at Cherokee Street. You can make the 2.5-mile trip in less than an hour, but I had a stop planned.

The route would take me through the Tower Grove South neighborhood, which changes considerably as you head south to north. Early on, I passed apartment buildings, old houses, a handful of small churches, and some used car lots. Then I crossed the bridge over the railroad tracks that cut through South City. To the left, I took in a splendid view of the domed building over the St. Louis Forensic Treatment Center South. The other side of the tracks

The Vintage Haberdashery

presented a different scene, filled with a variety of pubs, restaurants, specialty shops, and apartments—many housed in refurbished and new buildings. At Connecticut Street, three sets of plastic women's legs stand inside a second-floor window. I had always wondered about this, so I moseyed into the vintage clothing store below called the Vintage Haberdashery. Owner Jolie Mackney told me the legs belong to her. She decorates them with Halloween-themed tights in October and Christmas tights in December. Jolie is an original, and so is her store. In addition to vintage apparel, she offers period clothing for sale or rent. On the same side of Morgan Ford stands the Amsterdam Tavern. The drinks, sandwiches, and burgers notwithstanding, the tavern is best known for airing European football (soccer, as we know it) in the early morning on weekends. Major tournaments like the World Cup draw hordes of internationals and locals from all over the metro area.

When I would drive through this stretch of Morgan Ford just two decades ago, I'd seldom stop (except at South Side Mower Repairs for an annual mower tuneup), because the businesses generally attracted a questionable clientele. Since then, the hard work of business leaders slowly but surely turned the area around, so much so that new housing has cropped up. Catty corner to the Vintage Haberdashery is the MoFo Urban Residences at Connecticut Street and Morgan Ford. The new 26-unit apartment building replaced a car wash and stands next to a trailblazing operation called the Road Crew Coffee and Cycles, where, in one stop, you can sip a latte and shop for bicycle equipment. Owner Chris Green used to work at a bike shop before he opened Road Crew in October 2019. On one side, customers talk with friends and work on laptops, and the other features everything bicycles, including parts and service. Bicycles are seasonal items, Green told me. By adding coffee, he brings in revenue throughout the year.

Farther down Morgan Ford, as I passed a variety of active storefronts, I came across another unique establishment. The Local Harvest Grocery, open since 2007, favors items produced within 150 miles. Grass-fed beef, eggs and dairy products yielded without hormones or antibiotics, artisanal foods, and other regional items pack the place. The popular store abuts the neighborhood's longest-operating business, yet another bike shop. This one—A&M Cyclery—has called Morgan Ford home since 1929 and continues to serve the neighborhood despite having changed hands multiple times.

A&M marks the end of Morgan Ford and, appropriately, faces Tower Grove Park. Across from the park on Arsenal Street, you'll find some of the most attractive homes in the city. Construction of these charming, ample homes—featuring styles such as Craftsman Bungalow, Late Victorian, and Queen Anne—began in the years following the opening of the park in 1872. People from a variety of ethnic groups and income levels flocked to Tower Grove South after the start of the 20th century. Even after the neighborhood experienced decline post-World War II, passion for the neighborhood remained.

Interest from the outside steadily began to grow, as people took notice of the wide variety of nearby amenities, from Tower Grove Park itself to the international restaurants on South Grand Boulevard to everything Morgan Ford Road offers. The neighborhood offers the best of city living at an affordable price.

I admired the housing as I walked east on Arsenal. In two-and-a-half blocks, I reached Roger Place. I hadn't eaten breakfast yet and yearned for a break, so I went south a block on Roger, donned my mask, and opened the door of my go-to hangout—Hartford Coffee Company. One of the hardest parts of the pandemic was not being able to spend time there writing and socializing with friends.

Today, my needs were simple: two cookies and a large strawberry Italian soda. After getting my food, I sat at a table for one and read more of *The Broken Heart of America: St. Louis and the Violent History of the United States* by Walter Johnson. In this mighty 520-page doorstop, Johnson explains how just about every St. Louisan I once admired had helped to advance various kinds of racism. Many along my path for the day likely would have agreed with Johnson's assessment. When I returned to Arsenal, signs saying "Black Lives Matter" appeared on countless lawns. The calls for change seemed to reflect unity in residents' views and hopes.

They were also on the same page when it came to patronizing businesses on South Grand. Outside of MoKaBe's Coffeehouse near Grand, people filled the patio tables on this warm Sunday. I saw the same thing at the restaurants—like Tree House, Steve's Hot Dogs, and Rooster—on Grand. It was prime time for congregating.

Patio at Tree House on South Grand. Courtesy Jim Merkel

Decades ago, during a period of decline, real estate developers accurately predicted that the neighborhood would become vibrant again. One of the developers, David McCreery, owns property on the southwest corner of Grand and Arsenal, where streetcar lines once met. A key leader of the South Grand business district, McCreery recalled the desolation of the mid-to-late 1980s. For example, he seldom saw a woman pushing a baby stroller in nearby Tower Grove Park before the park's administration made big changes to prompt a turnaround. When McCreery first bought the building at Grand and Arsenal, tenants included the Socialist Party, which distributed material funded by the government of the Soviet Union. He also rented to the Rosicrucians, a group that claims to study and practice the natural laws of the universe. The building now features popular establishments like MoKaBe's, Hotbox Cookies, and Dunaway Books, specializing in used and rare publications. Heading south on Grand, you can find everything from records to natural foods to some of the best restaurants in the city. International offerings abound on this stretch, with a dozen or more nationalities represented. Parts of the world include Ethiopia, Turkey, China, Italy, France, Japan, Vietnam, the Philippines, Morocco, Brazil, Lebanon, and Persia, among others.

The King and I was scheduled to move to Richmond Heights in the spring of 2023, but stands out as a pioneer on South Grand. At 23, Suchin Prapaisilp came to St. Louis from Thailand

International Institute in the 1940s.
Courtesy Missouri Historical Society, St. Louis

in 1975 and six years later opened the restaurant on 3157 South Grand Boulevard. He also was a pioneering owner of a Lebanese eatery and the co-founder of Jay International Foods at 3172 South Grand. According to Prapaisilp, low rents brought international restaurants to this district. He also credits the International Institute, now located just a few blocks east of Grand on Arsenal. The organization has provided job placement and other assimilation services to immigrants since 1919.

As I continued south on Grand, I noticed that the stretch of shops and restaurants thin out at Humphrey Street. The next block is Utah Street, where to the west, stately homes face streets separated by a landscaped median (marking the entrance to the Tower Grove Heights neighborhood), and to the east, St. Pius V Catholic Church, a Romanesque building known for its mosaic and stained glass. I made my way to the Carpenter Branch of the St. Louis Public Library, where a half-dozen people waited for the place to open at 1 p.m. I called my wife and asked her to pick me up there. Just two blocks farther south, where Cherokee Street intersects with Grand, I would start my next walk on a different day. My Cherokee Street route would present another character-rich neighborhood but one with a markedly different personality.

St. Pius V

Cherokee Street

AN OLD SHOPPING DISTRICT STAYS ALIVE

Cherokee Street

L ong before shopping centers and malls came to life in the county, Cherokee Street was the place to shop in South City. Then city folks started driving to the malls beyond St. Louis's borders, and boards went up on many of those Cherokee Street stores. A sad ending? Not quite. The county malls started closing early in the 21st Century, but antique stores and Mexican restaurants and businesses sprouted in their place on Cherokee. This shopping district stayed alive, long after many had written its obituary.

Around 7:15 a.m. on September 20, my brother Charles and I began our tour of this revitalized street by walking east on Cherokee from Grand Boulevard. The first sighting of an antique store happens at Louisiana Avenue with the Bricoleur Arts, Antiques, and Repurposed Goods. This charming store features an array of unique and eclectic items, all thoughtfully curated. At the next cross street—Virginia Avenue—we saw a faded sign painted on the side of a brick building that says . . . Coca Cola? Something else? Beats me. The message on the side of the next brick building is clear enough: Cherokee Auto Parts.

Farther down, the brightest blues on the outside of the STL-Style House building somehow complement the yellows, oranges, reds, and other colors in this rich mural. To give their store a splash, owners Randy and Jeff Vines commissioned a mural on their store's Compton Avenue side by artist Robert Fishbone and his daughter Liza and his son Tyler Fishbone of On the Wall Productions. Features included brown columns, 1970s-style disco ball and even Frankie the Cat. The feline owned by the Vines hangs out at the place during business days and demonstrates who's boss.

Inside the store, from quality T-shirts to eye popping designs, STL-Style House exudes a passion for St. Louis and excellence. The Vines, who are identical twins, started selling T-shirts with St. Louis–centric design as a sideline in Dogtown back in 2001. When sales took off, they moved into their building at Compton and Cherokee and expanded their offerings to include posters, hats, socks, and totes. They added custom design, screenprinting, promotional products, and even masks decorated with the St. Louis flag. Their designs are fun and colorful, though some have expressions that aren't suitable for kids.

Lorraine and I have bought T-shirts at the shop for years, and I've held several book signings there. I recently discovered that the Vines' building once housed my great aunt Lillian's beauty shop, so I gave a photo of it to the Vines brothers. Decades ago, shops that met everyday needs were more common in the neighborhood, but today you'll find more destination stores that specialize.

STL-Style House

More stores mix with residences as we crossed Nebraska Avenue and reached the small, private Love Bank Park. The community owns the

Cherokee Street in the 1940s. Courtesy Missouri Historical Society, St. Louis

park and uses it for events like flea markets, bonfires, and art projects. Here, I encountered a chalkboard for anyone to mark up. Someone had taped a picture of a sad-looking, lost dog named Debbie and left a phone number to call if someone found her.

Moving farther east, we entered the Mexican district, where we encountered bigger buildings and bigger stores. Jason Deem, a community leader and developer, said Cherokee Street is one of the oldest continuously operating business districts in the city of St. Louis. In the 19th century, streetcars intersected at California Avenue and Cherokee. Merchants followed, and shoppers have come ever since. Branches of downtown department stores, shoe stores, and jewelers came to Cherokee Street, making it the downtown of the South Side. By 1956, the year before Crestwood Plaza opened, more than 110 merchants of different types served the public (you could find even more on side streets). The strip brimmed with life with just a handful of vacancies. You could buy groceries, get your hair permed, explore J. C. Penney and Woolworths, purchase a suit or dress, eat a burger, quaff a Budweiser, dance the night away, or shop for a wedding ring. Today, the shops often are quirkier, more offbeat. One is Diana's Bakery, a classic Mexican place where we perused sweet goodies.

Over time, Cherokee Street businesses lost steam, and the storefronts emptied. The Casa Loma Ballroom was the only holdout. As early as 1927 ballrooms existed at the current location, 3354 Iowa Avenue. The first establishments that occupied that space enjoyed limited success until 1935, when the Casa Loma Ballroom opened and flourished. A fire on a bitter cold evening on January 14, 1940, halted operation when it burned the building down, but in November of that year, the rebuilt Casa Loma opened to the sounds of Herbie Kaye and his orchestra. Over the years, Glenn Miller, Tommy Dorsey, Guy Lombardo, Duke Ellington, and Frank Sinatra entertained at this palace of sounds. Crowds of up to 2,000 filled the place back in its heyday. Now, about 200 show up to events on Friday, Saturday, and Sunday, said Pat Brannon, owner of the ballroom since 1990. These days, audiences experience big band, rock 'n' roll, burlesque, mixed martial arts, and wrestling. Wedding receptions and fundraisers also find a place in the Casa Loma. Brannon does his part to keep the venue up to date. He has invested $125,000 in sound, lights, and video.

Brannon is part of a group that worked to bring the street back after the strip declined in the mid-to-late 1960s, as suburban malls drew customers away. The comeback started around the 1990s, partly because storefronts were cheap to rent and because a vibrant Mexican community moved in. They brought shops and restaurants, as well as the annual Cinco de Mayo celebration.

The Carniceria Latino Americana, a Mexican grocery store and restaurant, opened at 2800 Cherokee Street in 1990. During the pandemic, the place owned by Carlos Dominguez consolidated to just a grocery store, but it still serves grilled chicken, tacos, burritos, special salsas, and other foods. Other Mexican businesses have joined Dominguez in offering an array of authentic fare not available in other parts of town.

From food to booze to art, the storefronts we passed heading east ranged widely. Finally, we reached Jefferson Avenue and faced the site of a piece of American kitsch. It had been a tall statue of a Cherokee Indian fashioned in 1985 by Bill Christman, a sculptor known for his wild artwork at the City Museum downtown. As the national mood grew against statues that some found offensive, a movement grew to remove the Indian. Even Christman wanted it down. He remarked that the Indian had the kitschy style of what you'd find in

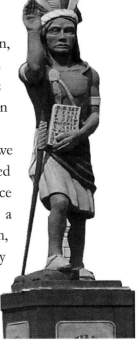

Courtesy Don Korte

a muffler store. After a vote, a community organization removed it in September 2021. In 2023, community leaders were raising money for a dignified statue by a Cherokee sculptor.

We crossed Jefferson Avenue, walked another block, and entered Antique Row. Here, the trees between street and sidewalk are taller, fuller, and cast a bigger shadow. Stores are fewer and farther between, as residences fill most of the blocks. The Cherokee-Lemp Special District helps oversee Cherokee Street eleven blocks east of Indiana Avenue (streets west of Indiana to Gravois are handled by the Cherokee Street Community Improvement). CLSD President Ray Simon, an architect and resident of the area, noted his organization's territory lacked the big retail stores found west of Jefferson, but it attracted smaller, more quaint shops, like antique stores.

Antiques remain popular along this stretch, like Elder's Antiques, one of the oldest establishments. Cherri Elder, who grew up in North City, has owned the store for decades and said that everyone in her family has worked there selling old treasures. Her kids paid their way through college moving furniture for Elder's on the weekend. Elder claimed she has seen and sensed spirits at the store, including the ghosts of a young girl and the late owner.

Other quirky and fun places appear along Antique Row. Lovers of java and felines can imbibe their favorite espresso while picking out a cat to play with or adopt at the Cheshire Grin Cat Café; the geologically inclined can check out STL Rocks, which sells . . . rocks, in addition to crystal and sterling silver jewelry; and melophiles can find the kind of rock on vinyl at Dead Wax Records, known for a carefully curated selection and friendly customer service.

The neighborhood becomes industrial, or rather defunct industrial, as we approach the old William J. Lemp Brewery. The 14-acre complex slaked the city's thirst for beer with its Falstaff brand. After Prohibition began, the Lemps sold the Falstaff trademark to brewers Joseph Griesedieck and his son Alvin, who predicted the nation would eventually tire of forced sobriety and demand the reopening of taps. In 1922, the Lemps sold their facility at a fraction of its value to the International Shoe Company. Now called Lemp Brewery Complex, the property hosts a mix of artist studios, offices, industries, and warehouses, all under the shadow of a dormant smokestack.

Not far from Lemp stands the Chatillon-DeMenil House. Local experts in architectural history speak of its significance as one of the biggest Greek Revival homes in the city. The first part was built in 1849 as a farmhouse by Henri Chatillon, a hunter and guide for the American Fur Company of St. Louis. The next owner was a rich Frenchman, Dr. Nicholas DeMenil, and his wife Emily Sophie Chouteau, a descendant of St. Louis's founding family. They hired an architect to upgrade the building to its current grandeur. After their deaths, the building stayed in the DeMenil family and went into decline. The house's future looked bleak when Missouri originally mapped the route of what would become Interstate 55, running directly through the property. The Landmarks Association of St. Louis came to the rescue and bought the property from the state with a $40,000 gift from Union Electric (now Ameren). Enthusiast benefactors and donors also pitched in to restore the old mansion and dedicated it in 1965. Today, the mansion hosts popular historic tours and events. When I go, I like to look at the piano made by my great-great grandfather, Louis C. Merkel, which my father donated in the 1960s.

Farther down DeMenil Place is the Lemp Mansion Restaurant and Inn next to the Lemp Mansion. The property includes the restaurant, lodging, and an event space for weddings and mystery dinners. Much of the place's reputation

Chatillon-DeMenil Mansion

comes from the stories of four suicides by members of the Lemp family, who owned the mansion and the nearby Lemp Brewery.

Success came to Johann Adam Lemp after he arrived in St. Louis in 1838. His brewery grew big and strong, but sorrow dogged his descendants. William J. Lemp Sr. shot himself in 1904, and his daughter Elsa Lemp Wright killed herself in 1920. Overcome by the loss of the brewery in 1922, Lemp Sr.'s son William J. Lemp Jr. also killed himself. Finally, a third child of William Sr., Charles Lemp, killed himself in the Lemp house in 1949. Some say these events make the mansion haunted, but I wonder whether some of it may be due to a family history of depression.

We walked to South Broadway so I could tap my foot on the street, which completed the walk. My brother and I then returned to Diana's Bakery, where we'd stopped earlier. I filled a bag with muffins and pound cake for Lorraine and me. Treats from a place like Diana's make any urban hike worthwhile.

Lemp Mansion
Courtesy Missouri Historical Society, St. Louis

Soulard Market

BEER, BOXING, AND FARMERS AT A MARKET

The Soulard Neighborhood

Around 75 years ago, the Soulard neighborhood looked so decrepit that supposedly wise city planners put it on a list for demolition. The area around the Anheuser-Busch brewery and the Soulard Farmers Market survived those attempts at destruction. Eventually, the hard work of Soulard's community resurrected the neighborhood and turned it into a jewel. These days, Soulard's bars, restaurants, and farmers market, along with its Mardi Gras Parade, attract folks from everywhere. On September 26, 2021, it drew me in for a walk.

After church, I rushed home and changed out of my Sunday best to jeans, a T-shirt, and shoes. I planned to walk through Soulard and continue through Lafayette Square. Just after noon, I stood at Cherokee Street and South Broadway with my phone and a plastic bag from Schnucks containing a chilled can of Raspberry Bubly Sparkling Water along with a bottle of water. My brother derides my use of plastic bags to carry stuff, but I hold my ground.

I stuck to what I know and set off north on Broadway. The area I passed through has a long history. In 1794, a Frenchman named Antoine Soulard came to St. Louis as the new surveyor-general of Upper Louisiana and fell in love with a woman named Julia Cerre. When they married the next year, Julia's father gave the couple a tract south of the village of St. Louis, the land now known as Soulard. It is also known for a mix of nationalities who later settled in the area, starting with the Germans in the 1830s. When political strife in Germany and the modern-day Czech Republic forced people to flee the countries in 1848, many Germans and Bohemians settled in Soulard. Italians, Serbians, Syrians, Hungarians, and Croatians also found refuge in the area, making homes in the two- and three-story brick houses, some of the earliest housing in St. Louis that reflects a distinct style. Soulard's houses are jammed closely together next to sidewalks and often have mansard roofs or sideways gable roofs with small dormers on top. One unusual structure in Soulard is the "half" house, where roofs descend sharply in one direction so rain can run off quickly. The neighborhood architecture possesses a grace that makes visitors want to come back again and again.

On my way to the heart of Soulard, I walked along Lyon Park and noticed a statue of Captain Nathaniel Lyon on his horse. Lyon, the commander of the St. Louis Arsenal at the start of the Civil War, achieved glory by forcing the surrender of a state militia group thought to be plotting a Confederate attack on Camp Jackson (located on the present-day campus of Saint Louis University). That surrender, made possible by the infusion of thousands of German volunteers, ended any possibility that St. Louis, and with it Missouri, would fight for the Confederacy during the Civil War. Lyon was promoted to brigadier general for his achievement, and in 1869, Congress donated 10 acres of the arsenal for a park named in memory of Lyon. A monument to Lyon in the form of an obelisk was installed five years later in the park, and a statue of Lyon, unveiled in 1929 in Camp Jackson Plaza near Saint Louis University, moved to the park in 1960.

Nathaniel Lyon had received help in his campaign from many St. Louis Germans, a group that also played a big part in the nearby Anheuser-Busch Brewery, where brewmasters make enough beer to fill Lake Superior. Outside of the Gateway Arch and Busch Stadium, the brewery may attract more tourists than any other building in St. Louis. Ever since the E. Anheuser & Co.'s Brewing Association introduced Budweiser in 1876, illustrations of the plant have played a role in company advertising. The plant received unprecedented attention the night of April 6, 1933, when a crowd of around 25,000 people celebrated the end of Prohibition at

Arsenal Street and South Broadway. The crowd cheered the dozens of trucks filled with Budweiser as they left the plant and delivered to the masses. Despite being owned by international interests as of 2008, the brewery continues to churn out a wide variety of products that A-B markets with gusto.

After admiring St. Louis's beer palace, I continued north and passed the point where South Broadway turns into Seventh Boulevard. Soon after, I reached the South Broadway Athletic Club at Shenandoah Avenue. The place has been a hotbed of activity since it started as a debate club on December 5, 1899. Over time, it expanded to include boxing and wrestling matches, not to mention gentler events like concerts, dances, softball, corkball, and washers. A few years ago, the club fell on hard times, but a new group of members brought the club back to life and finally allowed women to join as full members. Indeed, they always were a part, as daughters followed dads to events and later joined the auxiliary. But this was new.

Mike Button, club president from 1987 to 1996, told me that camaraderie has always helped keep the club going. Button was a teenager in the Soulard neighborhood in the 1960s and early 1970s when owners couldn't give property away. To Button, the club has always provided a social outlet for the neighborhood. He was a member long before he became president and practically raised his kids there. He's quick to point out that the club has produced boxers of national stature, like Mike Buha, who fought for the heavyweight championship of the world, or Billy Stephan, who boxed in Madison Square Garden. Pros seen on the old Wrestling at the Chase also practiced at the club, and you can still catch the occasional match there. If you go, you might find former neighborhood alderman Dan Guenther, a member and frequent volunteer, in attendance.

Heading further north on 7th, I eventually hit Russell Boulevard. To the west are popular local eating and drinking establishments like Hammerstone's, Tucker's Place, and—a popular destination for locals and tourists alike—John D. McGurk's Irish Pub and Garden. Be aware: the "Irish" isn't in McGurk's name just to get more customers on St. Patrick's Day. After an hour at this bar and grill, you'll expect to exit onto a street in Dublin. McGurk's began in 1978, when two local lawyers

bought a shuttered bar and broasted chicken place at 12th Street and Russell Boulevard. The owners called their place an Irish pub and played tapes of Irish music until they were told that to be authentic, they had to bring in Irish bands to play live music. Otherwise, they were just a bar.

The owners went all-in on the advice and hired groups from Ireland to perform. These days, half of the bands come from Ireland, and the other half include Irish expats who live in St. Louis. No matter who is playing, people flock to McGurk's for the best in Irish food, drink, and merriment.

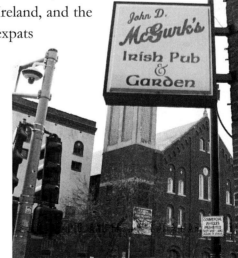

My route missed not only Soulard's famous night spots but also its distinctive and gorgeous homes. Jay Gibbs, a longtime neighborhood resident, filled me in over coffee at the Soulard Coffee Garden on Geyer Avenue. Gibbs said German immigrants built many of the neighborhood's brick homes from about 1845 to 1900. The neighborhood declined in the first half of the 20th century, but urban pioneers started bringing the place back around the early 1970s. The part they restored contains some of the earliest houses in St. Louis. Similar to housing in early American cities like Baltimore, dwellings in Soulard appear jammed together next to sidewalks. The land

The Historic Slezak House on Geyer Avenue in Soulard

was expensive, so builders made the lots narrow. They started building in the north part of the neighborhood around the Soulard Market and made their way south. About 5,000 souls live in Soulard today, but 30,000 to 60,000 people dwelt in the same space in the 19th century, when crowded conditions reigned.

In recent years, crowded conditions in Soulard have mainly taken over when people massed at its annual Mardi Gras parade. Many thousands come to the event, which starts at Busch Stadium, heads generally south on Seventh Street, and ends at the brewery. Attendees make memories of all varieties, some wilder than others. I love the parade route, because it takes me near the intersection of Park Avenue and Broadway. My great-great grandfather Louis C. Merkel—who made the piano at the Chatillon-DeMenil Mansion—lived there with his family after moving from New York in 1858, not long after he had immigrated from Germany. I'd like to think the revelers at the Mardi Gras parade are celebrating his arrival, but I know better.

The parade and subsequent street party started as a cooperative effort of local bars. Mike Button rode on a float in the first parade in 1979 and has been involved in floats for his club and for his family ever since. With all the crowds, Mardi Gras is one time for bars and restaurants to get ahead. The event appeals to a younger set of people but includes family features like the Cajun cookout and the Purina Pet Parade. Longtime area broadcaster Steve Potter has some dog-gone good memories of the pet parade, which he participated from 1990 until 2016, when his chihuahua Little Stevie Junior died. When he did come, he stayed the night at a friend's, where a bar and bathroom were always available.

When I walked away from the parade route and headed west on Lafayette, I noticed how quiet Soulard Market was. But it wasn't a Saturday, when throngs of people seek bargains on kale, fresh fish, baked bread, and various other items. Hundreds buy or sell at the Soulard Farmers Market. As I see it, the market is one of the most lively and colorful places around.

My experience on a different day affirmed this observation. Inside the market on the weekend, you'll find a sea of humanity and noise, not to mention fruits, vegetables, meats, and clothing. When I visited, apples, oranges, and other delights stood out, but so did ball caps emblazoned with "USA" or Cubs, Chiefs, and Superman logos. I checked out other vendors like Hermann Handmade Soaps and Jennifer's Meat & Fish. At Soulard Market, you can also find gourmet mushrooms, Bloody Marys, and roasted corn.

But not my books.

A few summers back, I spent two or three months in a stall selling my different books. Before the City would consider me, I paid for a business license, insurance, and a membership in the market association. It wasn't cheap. In addition, I paid a weekly fee of $40 ($30 outside of the summer). To get the best spot available, I arrived as early as 6 a.m. and set up my wares. Then I watched crowds walk past me to stalls with food and plants. I quit by mid-summer. A guy next to me who fried Lilliputian doughnuts told me he'd put himself through college with his Saturday yields. I was clearly in the wrong industry.

Leaving the market behind, I continued west on Lafayette Avenue and eventually heard a rumble after crossing 9th. The rumble turned into a roar as I crossed over Interstates 44 and 55. The

superhighway has five lanes in each direction and plenty of space for the vehicles that cram the roadway. The bridge marked the end of my two-mile walk. I would see more before the end of the day but needed some water first to deal with the heat and humidity. Nothing can oppress the spirit or spoil plans like hot days in St. Louis, whether you live on the south or any other side.

The bridge that crosses over Interstates 44 and 55

LIFE IN A MUSEUM

Lafayette Square

A s I walked west on Lafayette Avenue from the I-55 bridge on September 26, I encountered a busy Tucker Boulevard. I crossed the street and saw to my right a huge condo building that once housed the old City Hospital. To my left stood an 80-foot-tall, red sculpture that resembles enormous beams gathered together. Called *Treemonisha*, the work by artist John Henry pays tribute to the eponymous opera composed by Scott Joplin.

Before long, I reached the edge of the stunningly restored Lafayette Square—part neighborhood, part-museum. Lafayette Square came into existence in 1836 when the city decided to sell off the St. Louis Common (land jointly reserved in the previous century for public pastureland and related purposes). The city's deep pockets funded the design and construction of resplendent mansions that face Lafayette Park, named for the French general, the Marquis de Lafayette, who fought with the Americans in the Revolutionary War and visited St. Louis in 1825.

Aftermath of the 1896 tornado. Public domain

The dwellings that surrounded the park originally housed the richest of the rich in St. Louis. However, toward the end of the 19th century, the area started to deteriorate as the affluent moved west. Then, in 1896, a massive tornado made a direct hit on the neighborhood and dealt what seemed like a death blow. For decades, Lafayette Square remained rundown.

Fortunately for all of us, urban pioneers who recognized the beauty and importance of the homes helped bring the area back to life. The turnaround may have started in 1949, when preservationist John Albury Bryan bought a home on 21 Benton Place and restored it. Almost every home except Bryan's was in disrepair, but he spoke of the neighborhood's potential and invited rehabbers to join the restoration effort. Under the circumstances, Bryan may have seemed daft, but the results speak for themselves. Lafayette Square continues to win the recognition of local and national experts for historical significance. The neighborhood also is in the National Register of Historic Places.

You can tell the Second Empire–style Victorian townhouses in Lafayette by their windows, which often curve at the top; their mansard roofs; and their third floors. Made of red brick and stone, Romanesque revival dwellings fill the square, where you'll also find eclectic paint jobs as well as ornate wrought iron fences surrounding compact front yards.

The neighborhood's class and charm attracted residents then and still does today. One historic home was the abode of Horace E. Bixby, a riverboat pilot who befriended Samuel Clemens (Mark Twain). When the Civil War started, Bixby was named chief pilot of the Union Gunboat Fleet on the Mississippi and later inspired a character in Twain's book *Life on the Mississippi*.

A few doors down lived one of the neighborhood's restoration heroes. Ruth Kamphoefner lost her husband in 1964 and supported her five kids with Social Security checks and a part-time job as an art teacher. To save money, she bought a roach-infested shell on Mississippi Avenue and rehabbed it. Kamphoefner went on to restore homes throughout the neighborhood with unparalleled enthusiasm and became a leader in the renewal effort. She told her family's story in her self-published book *Lafayette Comes Back*.

Residents of Kamphoefner's block of Mississippi can see a wrought-iron fence across the street when they open their doors. An opening in the middle of the block serves as an entrance to Lafayette Park. Inside the park, statues of two early American politicians, both unveiled in the late 1860s, stand near the lake. One is of US Senator Thomas Hart Benton, who represented Missouri for three decades after it became a state in 1821 and famously claimed that a transcontinental railroad from St. Louis to San Francisco would lead to a Pacific empire. The statue, unveiled with 40,000 people watching,

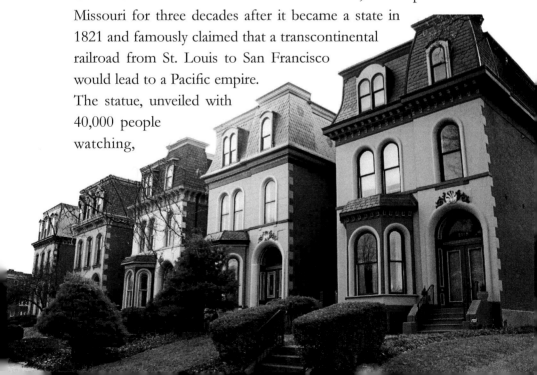

faces west and depicts Benton wearing explorer's boots and the toga of a Roman senator. The other statue—one of just six bronze castings made by French sculptor Jean-Antoine Houdon in 1792—depicts George Washington holding a bundle of rods upright. The City of St. Louis website describes the rendering as "the only likeness for which Washington ever posed."

Close by, the scenery could be described as dreamy. Weeping willows enshroud a dreamy grotto where an iron bridge crosses a lake. The scene resembles impressionist paintings or a pointillist work by George Seurat, which explains why many people have wedding photos taken here. The park is surely a gem overall but not too pristine for use. Formed in 2001, the Lafayette Park Conservancy works to preserve the park's historical character while encouraging use. Examples of the latter include band performances, a garden tour and art fair, a holiday market, and the annual Jim King Holiday Pet Parade. Bring your dogs, or, if you're brave, your cats.

After wandering the park, I returned to Mississippi Avenue and made my way to a busy area of merchants and restaurateurs along Park Avenue. Joggers ran and parents pushed strollers by active storefronts filled with a slew of businesses—a salon, realty office,

Lafayette Park

art gallery, wine shop, bar, and a café, where locals chatted inside and out over lattes. Across the street, and on the other side of a plaza with a fountain, is SqWires Restaurant and Market. The popular establishment adapted its name from the Western Wire Factory, once housed in the same building.

On a different day, I sat at a picnic table in the plaza and asked three neighborhood leaders why they thought Lafayette Square had become so successful. One of the leaders, Suzanne Sessions, who has lived in the neighborhood for nearly four decades, mentioned the stringent historic regulations. Tom Murphy, president of the Lafayette Square Restoration Committee, and Matt Negri, past president, mentioned the willingness of community members to volunteer for mundane tasks like picking up trash. All three emphasized residents' commitment to keeping the paint crisp and the gardens fresh.

I talked to a few others before I decided to resume my walk. I kept north on Mississippi toward Chouteau Avenue, passing Second Empire Victorian townhouses and more old factory buildings, many of them converted to lofts or condos. There are other historic homes along streets that intersect with Mississippi, but none rival the homes on the square in terms of magnificence. At Chouteau, I found apartments and condos under construction. A new and different area awaited, and I'd soon explore it.

The Grove's Mouse Sculpture
Courtesy Jim Merkel

WALKIN' ON K STREET

West on Chouteau Avenue and Manchester Avenue

I t was 1804, and the Americans had just taken over St. Louis and started making changes that still affect us today. Among other tweaks, they named the 12th street west of Broadway "K," the 12th letter of the alphabet. In 1826, the city gave K Street from present-day Wharf Street to Broadway the name Hazel. And in 1857, the city renamed the whole street Chouteau, for Auguste Chouteau, who co-founded St. Louis with Pierre Laclède Liguest. Today, Chouteau begins at Wharf Street, next to the Mural Mile collection of outstanding graffiti art. The street then heads west and north until it passes Mississippi Avenue, where my tour of Lafayette Square ended. By turning left, I started a new tour on Chouteau on October 16. Some restaurants were within view at Mississippi and Chouteau, but to the west were mainly big industrial buildings and the site of one of the most harrowing incidents in St. Louis in decades.

On a red-hot St. Louis day in June 2005, a pressure relief valve on a propylene cylinder ignited at the Praxair Distribution, Inc. Center at 2210 Chouteau. Soon, other cylinders ignited before launching into Lafayette Square and other surrounding areas. One person died of an asthma attack brought on by smoke and fumes. After that tragedy, neighbors and the city refused to let Praxair reopen, and the community concluded that high-end apartments were the best replacement for much of the company's former property. Some of those apartments were under construction as I walked by.

I went a block or so on Chouteau before my phone rang. My friend from church, Albert, had called wanting to pray. We usually call each other once a day to do this, but this time we couldn't hear each other and hung up, resolving to talk later. Then, through a chain link fence, I eyed a bunch of rusty old military jets and helicopters. The main airplane was on display at the corner of Cardinal and Chouteau avenues. I'd estimate there were a couple of dozen old airships and parts of old planes and helicopters on the property, where the owner also operates a truck repair shop. He told the *St. Louis Post-Dispatch* in 2017 that his collection includes various American jets and Soviet MiGs. Some people collect stamps. This guy likes to collect fighter jets.

A little farther down the road, the elevation rose, which made me tired, hungry, and thirsty. Fortunately, next to Grand, I neared a Captain D's and a Rally's. I chose the Rally's and ordered a gigantic lemonade and two apple pies for a buck each. I took my time eating them. To the south stood the Edward A. Doisy Research Center and, behind it, SSM Health Saint Louis University Hospital.

As far as I know, that hospital was the final abode of my friend Vic. Vic lived with his cat in a second floor apartment in Carondelet. He once worked 60-hour weeks assisting chefs at some of the best restaurants in town, until heart problems forced him to retire early and live on disability pay, only $1,300 a month. He got groceries at a food bank near his house and trusted in the Lord when money ran out before the end of the month. I loved talking and praying with him. He had a simple religion that often involved him pursuing a direct line. He'd say, "Jesus and me, we had a talk."

I started worrying about losing Vic after he got cancer. Larry—the church elder with Parkinson's who joined me on an earlier walk—brought him groceries every week. Vic ended up at SSM Health St. Louis University Hospital when COVID-19 cases were high overall, and the hospital didn't allow visitors. After that, Vic and I kept in touch by phone. As Vic got sicker, our calls got shorter. Then he stopped answering calls from Larry and me, and we couldn't figure out how he was doing. Vic had family members out of town, but I didn't know them. I presume he died. What else could have happened? On the other hand, I still have a strange, absurd feeling that Vic might not be dead, only missing in action, and that any day he might call and invite me to hang out with him at Burger King. It's hard to grieve that way, or to deal with the feelings of loss I still have.

My thoughts turned from Vic as I crossed Grand on the north side of Chouteau and found myself in a large, flat field. The only thing in that field was a park bench at a bus stop on Chouteau, which looked lonely and isolated that afternoon. I went to the south side of Chouteau again, passed trucking firms, and found myself on a bridge over railroad tracks, northwest of an antique water tower and south of a raised portion of Interstate 64, past which buildings and four cranes were clustered.

Chouteau goes east to west through the middle of a rapidly growing, 400-acre redevelopment area, resulting in lots of construction. The street is bounded by Compton Avenue on the east, 39th Street on the west, Laclede Avenue on the north, and Interstate 44 on the south. From 2017 to 2022, the St. Louis Midtown Redevelopment Corporation brought $1.3 billion-worth of completed or announced development. The redevelopment corporation—a joint venture of SSM Health and Saint Louis University—should bring vast change in a once-blighted area. So said Brooks Goedecker, the executive director.

I arrived at the end of a bridge and found myself in a different place. The street bent to the left and became Manchester Avenue. Chouteau continued as a smaller residential street north of Manchester before it stopped near the intersection of South Kingshighway Boulevard and Interstate 64. In the 19th century, it had the name New Manchester Road, because it led to the town of Manchester in St. Louis County. Vandeventer Avenue on the east side of Kingshighway and Southwest Avenue on the west side of Kingshighway made up Old Manchester Road.

Today, Manchester starts at the east end of the thriving Grove entertainment district. In front of me stood a seven-story, brick apartment building. Ahead, a neon sign hung over Manchester proclaiming "THE GROVE." The style would have been perfect for a movie theater's marquee. In fact, a movie theater called the

Manchester once operated at 4247 Manchester in the early and middle part of the last century.

Today, much is shiny, new, and colorful in the mile from Vandeventer Avenue to Kingshighway Boulevard. One of the first things I noticed were the many concrete balls along Manchester meant to slow down traffic. Before long, I came across an odd sculpture that resembled a mouse with its head and neck tilted to one side. The pose made my neck sore just looking.

Other works of art stand out in the Grove, including the murals. One looks like an old postcard, with each letter of the "GROVE" filled with a different scene. A different mural shows a gigantic Cardinal in the middle of a city landscape, while another uses the intense face of a black cat to promote Firecracker Pizza.

Brian Phillips, the assistant vice chancellor and executive director of the Washington University Medical Center Redevelopment Corporation, said the neighborhood was a busy, blue-collar area inhabited by about 11,500 people in 1950. It boasted a shopping district called the Manchester Strip and attracted people from all over the city. The neighborhood declined during the next few decades, and by the year 2000, the population had shrunk to about 2,000. The Grove began making a comeback after Washington University started investing in the area and an influx of LGBTQ establishments attracted more people. The Grove is proud of its LGBTQ story; rainbow flags appear in storefront windows and fly outside of buildings along Manchester. According to Phillips, the

LGBTQ community gravitated here because Forest Park Southeast was more welcoming than other communities.

HandleBar

Just west of Just John Nightclub (and across the street) is HandleBar. Its owner is Tatyana Telnikova, a Russian immigrant who opened the place when many stores were still boarded up. Over the years, she has seen her bar's business and the neighborhood grow together. Telnikova maintains that what happened in the Grove was the result of an organized and consistent effort. Street art in the Grove, including the bollards, the mouse, and the murals, has enhanced the neighborhood's unique flavor. She lauds the work of the area's Community Improvement District, a group formed by businesses and property owners to promote the Grove. She serves on the board and manages the group's marketing committee.

One property owner is developer Guy Slay, who bought a building at the southeast corner of Manchester and Tower Grove, restored it, and gave it the name Mangrove. Once, it housed the popular Carps Department Store, which attracted shoppers from The Hill and other nearby neighborhoods. Carps and other stores started to disappear around 1970. In 2005, Robbie Montgomery, a one-time backup singer for Ike and Tina Turner, opened a branch of her Sweetie Pie's soul food restaurant in the location. She prospered so much that lines to enter often curved around the block. People from around the world dropped by to try Montgomery's soul food.

Then Oprah Winfrey heard about the place, which led to Welcome to Sweetie Pie's, a reality show that aired on Oprah's network. However, Sweetie Pie's popularity dwindled after an ugly event, when Montgomery's son and co-star, James "Tim" Norman, was convicted on federal murder-for-hire charges in the death of his nephew Andre Montgomery Jr., Robbie's grandson. According to prosecutors, Norman had hoped to collect as much as $450,000 of life insurance he had purchased on Andre. Travell Anthony Hill, whom Norman hired to shoot Montgomery, pleaded guilty to two murder for hire charges, and was sentenced to 32 years in prison. Terica Ellis pleaded guilty to one count of conspiracy to commit murder for hire and was sentenced to committing murder-for-hire.

After Sweetie Pie's left that location, another popular eatery eventually moved in. Grace Meat + Three has achieved national acclaim for its Southern fare and friendly counter service. I made a mental note to try it out on a different day, in part because of

Grace Meat + Three

crowds from an event taking place just down the street at Urban Chestnut, where traffic was blocked off for Oktoberfest St. Louis. Lines were long for the porta potties and the beer taps while a German band played on the raised platform of the Urban Chestnut Grove Brewery and Bierhall. There must have been thousands in the crowd.

I decided not to linger and kept west until I reached the far end of the festivities at Taylor Avenue. Behind me, above the street, hung another one of those neon signs that said "THE GROVE." In a couple of blocks, I'd be at Kingshighway. Then I'd turn right and travel to the end of my walk at Oakland Avenue. But first, I would pass the office of Park Central Development, which played a key role in bringing back the Grove. Formed in 2010, it provides community development services in 10 neighborhoods in St. Louis. In the Grove, the district funds services like beautification, safety, and infrastructure. It's one of many forces that have helped turn around the neighborhood. If an individual can get credit as a force, anyone who knows the history of the Grove would credit William

Danforth. The eventual chancellor of Washington University, Danforth was vice chancellor for medical affairs at the School of Medicine and president of the school's vast medical center from 1965 to 1971.

In 1970, Danforth started investigating ways to keep the medical school and its affiliated hospitals in their location in St. Louis. For the plan to work, he decided the city had to stabilize the surrounding area. His tool would be the Washington University Medical Center Redevelopment Corporation, an organization that worked with other groups to build and maintain neighborhoods like the Grove. Their success speaks for itself—the city has become more vibrant and held onto an invaluable medical hub for residents. Steins up for the Grove!

Turtle Park

ON THE ROAD OF TAMM AND THE AVENUE OF OAKS

Oakland Avenue, Tamm Avenue, and Manchester Avenue

P eople on the south side of Forest Park were surrounded by so many oak trees that they named an adjacent street Oakland Avenue. Over the years, Oakland Avenue has played host to several notable entertainment spots from South Kingshighway to Skinker Boulevard. Since the mid-1930s, they have faced a mighty highway referred to as both Interstate 64 and Highway 40. Before it became an interstate, the road from Skinker Boulevard to Vandeventer Avenue was called the Express Highway, or the Oakland Express Highway, because of its position just north of Oakland Avenue. Then in 1948, the Board of Aldermen changed its name to the Red Feather Express Highway, after the red feather symbol of the Community Chest charitable organizations. Alderman J. Ray Weinbrenner mocked the title and sought to change the name to Easter Bunny Lane or White Feather Highway "to indicate the attitude of this board on many issues."

The endless rush of cars along I-64/US 40 provided a monotonous soundtrack for my westward walk on Oakland

Avenue starting at Kingshighway on October 22. The first cross street I noticed was Lawn Place, a residential street. Kids who lived on the street in the early to mid-20th century must have loved being so close to exciting attractions of

the past like the Forest Park Highlands and the Arena. To get to either, those kids would have passed St. Louis University High School, an elite institution founded by the Jesuits. The all-boys school, founded at a different location in 1818, provides a first-rate education supported by a "men for others" mantra.

A different kind of institution stands just to the west of St. Louis University High. The St. Louis Science Center seeks to inspire scientific minds of all ages with a range of exhibits and attractions. One of the oldest features of the Science Center is the planetarium just across the highway in Forest Park. Designed like a giant white spacecraft, it has hosted astronomy exhibits and displays since the 1960s. Visitors can reach it using a walking

The James S. McDonnell Planetarium

bridge that crosses over the highway, visible at different spots in the flooring through plexiglass. The building on the Oakland side is decades newer.

A bit west of the center is where Stan Musial held court at the popular Stan Musial and Biggie's restaurant. With seafood, steaks, Italian food, prime rib, and frequent visits by Musial to schmooze diners, the eatery prospered. That part of Oakland Avenue was a hot spot, especially with Forest Park Highlands Amusement Park and the Arena just down the street. For more than 60 years, the 14-acre Highlands drew kids and grownups with features like a pool, a dance hall, and The Comet roller coaster. The park went up in flames on July 19, 1963, and the ferocious blaze destroyed most

Courtesy Missouri Historical Society, St. Louis

of the attractions. Not long after the fire, the property gave way to St. Louis Community College at Forest Park, which operates to this day. The college keeps that stretch of Oakland busy but can't match the excitement generated by the Highlands.

In a walk that began on October 22, I passed the college property and soon entered what used to be the parking lot for the famed Arena. Oldsters remember the Arena as a massive entertainment venue that held a wide variety of shows, concerts, and sporting events. Nicknamed the "old barn," it was built in 1929 to hold livestock and other agricultural shows. Over the next 70 years, it hosted everything from basketball, soccer, and hockey games, professional wrestling events, and circuses to the Rolling Stones and Michael

Public domain

Jackson. The Three Stooges entertained at the Arena and Ronald Reagan campaigned there (although not at the same time). Also, the first flight of a cow landed near the venue on February 18, 1930. The plane carrying the half-ton bovine took off from Bismarck, Missouri, and flew 72 miles to the International Aircraft Exposition at the Arena. In the name of science, somebody milked the animal midflight.

After the Arena became less viable as a major venue, the place shuttered in the 1990s. The bitter end came when construction finished on its replacement, the Kiel Center (now the Enterprise Center) downtown. On February 27, 1999, *Suburban Journals* photographer Dennis Caldwell and I were on assignment in the middle of a crowd behind the building to watch its implosion. Sadness filled the air as we witnessed the dramatic collapse of the Arena and all the fun it had courted through the years.

Today, offices and lofts fill the space left open by the Highlands and the Arena. Just down the block, near the corner of Hampton Avenue, a Mercedes-Benz dealership fills another gap left by the departure of a mainstay: KTVI studios. The site gained unwanted attention in the early morning of February 10, 1959, when a tornado roared through the neighborhood and sent the KTVI antenna crashing through the roof of the Arena. The twister, which started at Manchester Avenue and Brentwood Boulevard, took the lives of 21 St. Louisans. The city eventually recovered and so did KTVI, operating at its Hampton location for years afterward before moving much farther west to Maryland Heights.

On the other side of Hampton Avenue, the Evangelical Deaconess Society of St. Louis opened Deaconess Hospital in 1930. The hospital operated at Hampton and Oakland for more than a half-century before changing hands multiple times and eventually closing in 1997. The Saint Louis Zoo acquired the property in 2014 and plans to use the land to expand its grounds.

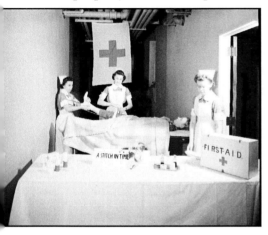

Deaconness Hospital. Courtesy the State Historical Society of Missouri

After reaching the old hospital site, I decided to stop for the day, after exactly 48 minutes, 34 seconds. I began the second half of my jaunt at Tamm Avenue and Oakland on October 15th. It lasted four seconds longer than the first half. (I guess I lost a step or two between walks.) Where I resumed, my walk spanned the north end of the northern segment of Tamm Avenue, named for a farmer, Jacob Tamm. The street was part of land originally granted to Charles Gratiot in 1797. Not long after that, President Thomas Jefferson commissioned a Scotsman named John Bradbury to study the nearby rivers. While he was in the region, Bradbury discovered the area around today's Dogtown contained rich deposits of coal and clay. This find helped clay mining become a major industry in the city.

At Oakland and Tamm is at a park known for fun concrete turtles. Kids and grownups climb over turtles that range from 7 to 40 feet long. Called Turtle Park, the place emerged from the quirky and eclectic mind of Bob Cassilly, the late founder of the famed City Museum downtown. The slightly absurd character of the animals are in keeping with the comic tone of the City Museum.

Pat Connolly Tavern. Courtesy Jim Merkel

If I hadn't spent time exploring Turtle Park that day, I would have gone to the Pat Connolly Tavern across the street. A sign for the tavern declares its loyalty to Dogtown and features a bottle of Tullamore Dew Irish Whiskey. Co-owner Joe Jovanovich remarked that St. Patrick's Day is among his busiest times of the year. He and his workers get up early, work through the evening, and then try to put Humpty Dumpty back together again.

Pat Connolly bought the place in 1942 and opened a tavern. The business has changed ownership multiple times, but Joe Jovanovich and his mother Teresa Connolly brought it back to the Connolly family in 2015. Three generations of the Connolly-Jovanovich family have been involved with the business, famous not just for beer but also for their fried chicken. The Connolly-Jovanovich family announced in 2023 that it was selling the business. Pat's is located close to the starting point of the annual St. Patrick's Day Dogtown Parade and Irish Festival. Under the sponsorship of the Ancient Order of Hibernians, the parade began in Clayton in 1984, moved to Hazelwood in 1985, and then to Dogtown in 1986. The celebration has been a permanent fixture in Dogtown since, except during 2020 and 2021 because of the pandemic. At the parade, many dozens of floats, fire trucks, and other vehicles participate. The caravan moves south on Tamm to its end point at Manchester, but the party continues into the evening.

Alibi Cookies is another of many businesses along the parade route. The shop stays open during parade day to witness and welcome the crowds. Mike Evans, the owner, moved to Dogtown in 2004 and started his store in 2020. A former chef and event DJ, Evans notes that customers gravitate to his cookie vending machine, which dispenses warm treats 24 hours a day to anyone with a craving. Evans came up with the idea to keep business going during the pandemic, and it stuck. Where else can you find a warm cookie at 3 a.m.?

The Dogtown neighborhood has a rich history, and lifelong residents Bob Corbett and his brother John have done much

Dogtown's St. Patrick's Day Parade in 2018.
Courtesy Jim Merkel

of the work of preserving it. Bob's a retired Webster University professor. John is the president of the Dogtown Historical Society and a retired University City firefighter. Like all historians, they love to use their research to demolish urban legends. They dispute, for example, the story that the area was named Dogtown because Igorots from the Philippines searched the neighborhood for pet dogs to eat during the 1904 World's Fair. In their research, the Corbetts found references to the word Dogtown in newspaper articles that ran before the fair. An article from 1889, for example, used the name while reporting that a kid living in the neighborhood told police that a murder had occurred there. Also, miners like the ones who lived in the area were called "dogs." Regardless, the official name of the neighborhood that includes Tamm from Oakland to Manchester isn't Dogtown, it's Clayton-Tamm.

The Corbetts' research also showed that Dogtown was never really an Irish enclave, as many people have assumed through the years. In fact, the Corbetts studied the nationality of Dogtown residents around 1900 and concluded that the Irish didn't even make up a majority. Census records from 1900 showed that the Irish were only slightly more numerous than the next biggest group, the French. Other groups that settled here included the English and Croatians. However, pastors of St. James the Greater Catholic Church from the 1860s to 1952 came from Ireland. They likely taught all parishioners the Irish way which is likely a big reason why people associate Dogtown with all things Irish.

I considered that connection again six months after my walk through the neighborhood, when I sat at a table with John Corbett at Seamus McDaniel's, a neighborhood staple at 1208 Tamm. We talked about the 1959 tornado, which also nailed Dogtown. Corbett often thinks about that storm because he was there. He recalled how the tornado ripped off the roof of a nearby house in the 6400 block of Wade Avenue and dropped it on top of another house.

It's bad enough when neighbors refuse to cut their grass. Worse still is when they leave their roof on your house. Fortunately for both sets of neighbors, John Corbett reported, the covering was returned to the original home, where it remains today. The tornado also smashed part of the new St. James School building and even struck a skate park, which sent roller skates everywhere. John Corbett was among the kids who ended up with free skates and used them to roll around the neighborhood.

Dogtown survived the tornado and bustles with activity these days. Modern stores and apartments fill the area around Seamus's. Along Tamm south of Clayton, you can find or repair a guitar, talk with an insurance agent, or get a custom frame. The storefronts steadily dwindle as you head farther south, but looming large on the west side of Tamm is the church of St. James the Greater.

Perched on a hill, the English Gothic Revival structure overlooks the parish's former school campus across the street. A decline in attendance forced the school to close in 2019, so the parish converted the building to a center that offers space for meetings, office use, fundraisers, and celebrations. The center still connects with the church in spirit; a Celtic cross on the front lawn honors the parish pastors of years past.

Walking by St. James, I came to a stretch of homes lining Tamm. I noticed multiple houses decorated with various Halloween ghosts, witches, and other spooky things. Continuing my trek down a long slope, I finally arrived at Manchester. My route turned left, and Halloween-themed houses turned into used car lots, which seemed to appear everywhere. On the south side of Tamm, train tracks run parallel with the street, which accounts for the factories and warehouses adjacent. The area feels downright industrial.

I passed under the Hampton Avenue Bridge and was photographing a business behind a fence with my phone, when a man showed up on the other side of a gate nearby and sternly asked what I was doing. Another man drove up soon after and asked the same thing. Fortunately, my car was close, so I hurried to it and drove off. Several days later, I accidentally dropped my phone into a washing machine and wiped out all the pictures I'd taken for this book. The men who'd asked what I was doing had nothing to worry about.

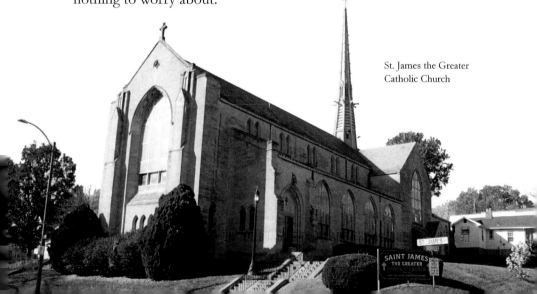

St. James the Greater
Catholic Church

St. Ambrose Catholic Church

ALL THINGS ITALIAN

The Hill

The environment of The Hill neighborhood traces to the mines of fireclay in the 1800s, which operated in an area that included Manchester Avenue near Sublette Avenue. That Cheltenham District encompassed what's now called The Hill and included the "King's Highway" at the eastern end of the neighborhood. Quakers from England built the first plant to process fireclay in St. Louis in 1844. When a new stop was added on the Pacific Railroad in 1852, the railroad provided a new way to bring bricks to the St. Louis market. Other mines followed and soon attracted impoverished Italians from the other side of the Atlantic. Many of these immigrants settled on The Hill, including Italians from both the northern Lombardy area and the southern area of Sicily. The two groups looked down on each other at the start, but the foundation of the neighborhood, St. Ambrose Catholic Church, drew the Lombards and Sicilians together to form one community.

The Italian neighborhood grew and has maintained its heritage ever since, which inspired a recent, award-winning documentary called

America's Last Little Italy: The Hill. On a walk through the neighborhood, I encountered endless examples of Italian heritage. Dozens of fantastico restaurants, groceries, bakeries, and delis provide the best Italian foods anywhere in the city. You'll come across spotless homes as well as clubs for an Italian game called bocce. Sports history runs deep here and not just with bocce. Not one but two Baseball Hall of Famers grew up across from each other on Elizabeth Avenue: catcher Yogi Berra and broadcaster Joe Garagiola. Another member of the Baseball Hall of Fame, Jack Buck, lived several doors down for a while. The coincidence inspired the city to give the 5400 block of Elizabeth Avenue the honorary designation "Hall of Fame Place." Football star Ben Pucci, another neighborhood kid, didn't reach the football hall of fame but played for the 1948 All-American champion Cleveland Browns.

And, of course, there's soccer. Fans remember that four Hill residents, and another south St. Louisan, helped the United States beat England in a colossal upset in the 1950 World Cup. That feat inspired a movie called *The Game of Their Lives*, some of which was filmed on The Hill.

In many ways, The Hill today is the same as it was then. Residents still relax on their porches and talk to friends passing on the sidewalk, and streets are still lined with vertical banners on light poles, serving as flags for the neighborhood. Matching the Italian colors, they're green at the top, white in the middle, and red at the bottom. Fire plugs are also painted green, white, and red. With these colors everywhere, residents of Rome, Naples, or Florence who find themselves on The Hill might wonder if they really are back home.

If those native Italians entered The Hill the way I did, they would have come in on Sublette Avenue at Manchester. My walk

Sacred Heart Villa

began at that intersection on October 29, and I made my way past train tracks and a factory district that includes a few businesses that process Italian food. I reached the residential part of the neighborhood after passing underneath a highway bridge where I-44 travelers sped by overhead. With me were my brother, who lives on The Hill, and two of his friends from Kansas City, Steve and Hanna Fuller. Steve is a municipal judge in North Kansas City and Hanna is a yoga instructor.

I walked a few more blocks before turning left at Wilson Avenue. Continuing down Wilson, I eventually arrived at Sacred Heart Villa, a Catholic preschool and kindergarten founded by the Apostles of the Sacred Heart of Jesus. The building once housed Cor Jesu Academy, an all-girls, Catholic high school that moved to Affton in 1965. The current campus, impeccably maintained, features a grotto and a statue of Mary.

There's no shortage of statues of Mary on The Hill. I came across many as I headed south on Edwards, where narrow brick and wooden homes called shotgun houses line multiple blocks. The story goes that the label "shotgun" suggests that a person could pull the trigger of a shotgun at the front door and watch the ammo exit cleanly out the back. The structures fit on narrow lots that allow for more homes per block. According to

LynnMarie Alexander, a third-generation resident of The Hill, most of these homes started with just one room, and families added more rooms over time. While you can find shotgun houses throughout The Hill, new property owners have torn down some and replaced them with new, larger homes.

We turned south on Edwards Street. The more we walked, the more homes changed. We turned left at Southwest Avenue and you could see the Arch in the distance. Our route went toward the monument briefly before taking me north and back into the neighborhood at Marconi Avenue, which we followed to the popular Italia-America Bocce Club. The game starts with the tossing of a *pollino*—a small ball used as a target on a 13-foot-wide by 91-foot-long court. Competitors roll bocce balls toward the pollino and whoever gets closest scores points. The bocce club, boasting more than 500 members, hosts games regularly, not to mention the National Federation of Bocce Clubs Tournament every four years. In 2019, they hosted an international friendly tournament.

Like many locals, Dea Hoover, a tour operator and author, spends time off work playing bocce at the club. Hoover, who joined in 2012, said the game is quieter than bowling, which means you can talk to others while playing. It reminds her of the game of pool, which her dad played when she was growing up. She ranks her skill-level as average.

Hoover said that by joining the club, she was able to meet many people from the neighborhood's Catholic Church, St. Ambrose, just a block north on Marconi. I went to St. Ambrose after visiting the bocce club. A wedding was letting out, and I saw friends and family of the new couple joyously celebrating. In a day that had been alternating between brilliant and overcast, the sky was now a bright blue. Those leaving the church likely noticed artist Rudolph Torrini's bronze statue *The Italian Immigrants*. The sculpture depicts a humble family starting life in America: a woman cuddles a baby while her husband holds a small suitcase. Another of Torrini's sculptures, *A Boy and His Dog*, appears on Tamm Avenue in Dogtown.

Torrini taught at Webster College in the 1960s, before it became Webster University. My sister took his art classes and learned a lesson in humility from him. Like many of his students, she came equipped with what she thought artists should have: an oversized canvas and a toolbox that doubled as a purse and a place to hold her paints. But Torrini reminded his students that what they looked like didn't make them artists; their art did. Torrini sounds

The Italian Immigrants statue outside of St. Ambrose. Courtesy Jim Merkel like just another guy, similar to the people in his statues.

Milo's Bocce Garden. Courtesy Jim Merkel

Catty-corner from St. Ambrose is Milo's Bocce Garden, owned by city alderman Joseph Vollmer, boss and chief dispenser of the brew. People from all over the metro area gather at Milo's, but the newest attraction stands directly across the street from St. Ambrose. The elegant Piazza Imo is an Italianate courtyard with a magnificent, white-marble fountain in the middle. Ed and Marge Imo of the Imo's pizza chain were significant contributors in an effort that involved support on and off The Hill. A bevy of bricks fills the piazza's walking paths, many of which are engraved with the names of donors.

Visitors often toss coins into the fountain, imported by the Frisella family from Italy. The lower pool of the fountain includes 96 jets that shoot water into the pool above. The sight is stunning at night when lights reflect off the white marble. When you're not tossing coins, you can rest on one of the benches nearby. On warm summer nights, my brother, my wife, and I like to sit just outside the piazza and enjoy gelato from the adjacent Gelato Di Riso. We sometimes see people playing chess inside the piazza at tournament-size chess tables donated by the St. Louis Chess Club, or we'll notice visitors admiring one of the religious statues that surround the courtyard.

Piazza Imo

A strongly Catholic area, The Hill has been supported by pastors and other leaders of St. Ambrose who have worked closely with the community to keep the neighborhood vibrant. In the early 1970s, then-associate pastor Salvatore Polizzi led the effort to minimize the disruption of the passage of the new Interstate 44 through the neighborhood. Together, residents of The Hill succeeded in getting an overpass built over I-44 at Edwards Street.

Polizzi developed a reputation as a caretaker of the neighborhood. His departure paved the way for Monsignor Vincent Bommarito, another charismatic leader. Known for his concise masses and thoughtful homilies, Bommarito kept the parish healthy for decades. In an interview, Bommarito recalled that at one time, there was tension between the residents and restaurant owners who occupied the same blocks. Businesses started buying up homes to turn them into parking spaces. These days, Bommarito notes, the eateries are comfortable with the residents and the residents are comfortable with the eateries. But Bommarito is concerned about the skyrocketing price of homes. One resident, my brother, anticipates he will one day be priced out of his little apartment. In the neighborhood's east side, the development company Draper and Kramer built a 225-unit apartment building, while McBride & Sons built up to 58 homes.

Bommarito said the growth benefits the St. Ambrose School, enabling the school to hire more quality teachers and to improve its education. Today, some of the kids in St. Ambrose Elementary School are fifth-generation attendees. The school opened in 1906 at 2110 Cooper Street with an auditorium and a classroom for first through fourth grade. Pushed by the Roman Catholic Archdiocese of St. Louis, it expanded to include fifth through eighth grade.

School may be important, but The Hill lives and dies on good, rich food, mostly influenced by the two regions—Lombardy and Sicily—represented by most of The Hill's population. Few blocks in the neighborhood lack a restaurant, bakery, or small grocery.

Good Italian restaurants appear everywhere, but what attracts many to The Hill on a Saturday are the places where you can buy ingredients for a great meal at home. The long list of purveyors include DiGregorio's Italian Market at Daggett and Marconi Avenues, where I found shelf after shelf of groceries from Italy. The store also displays numerous varieties of Italian wines and offers its own brands of sausages, olive salad, and other foods made from family recipes.

Tony Ribaudo, a DiGregorio family member who works at the market, estimates that 90 percent of that store's customers come from outside The Hill. Many stop at the store while they're in town attending a Cardinals-Cubs game, and others order from the website.

The DiGregorios have a large family but one branch of it spells the name with an "e" (DeGregorio). On a warm weather day, you might find Joe DeGregorio giving tours of The Hill or talking about his book about the neighborhood. According to his family story, Joe's grandfather was named Joseph DiGregorio when he immigrated to America. But when it was time to become a citizen, a judge pronounced the name DIE-Gregorio. Told he'd mispronounced the name, the judge suggested changing the spelling of DiGregorio to DeGregorio. The revision stuck.

On his tours, DeGregorio likes to point out businesses that produce specialty Italian meats like Oldani's Salumeria and Volpi Foods. Another establishment, Gioia's Deli, is known for its hot salami, or *salume de testa*, which helped garner the business a James Beard 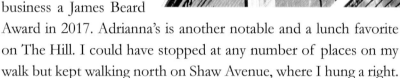 Award in 2017. Adrianna's is another notable and a lunch favorite on The Hill. I could have stopped at any number of places on my walk but kept walking north on Shaw Avenue, where I hung a right.

At the corner of Marconi is a familiar place: Shaw's Coffee, Ltd. I've been going there for years, as has my publisher, Josh Stevens. Not one to do business at his office, he loves to meet there with employees, clients, and (sometimes) me as he sips an Americano.

According to Alexander, many who visit The Hill for meals don't realize that the distinct food traditions of Lombardy and Sicily influence different restaurants. Lorenzo's, for example, serves northern Italian cuisine, while Gian-Tony's offers southern Italian/Sicilian cuisine. In northern Italy, at the base of the Alps, the diets are based on dairy cattle. They also eat large amounts of potatoes and rice, which both grow in the region. Sicilians, however, incorporate more seafood, not to mention more olive oil, lemons, olives, and tomatoes.

Regional influences aside, Joan Aiazzi—the owner of Rigazzi's—pointed out to me that each Italian eatery on The Hill has its own specialties. Her restaurant started in 1957 when two partners, John Riganti and Louis Aiazzi, went into business and combined parts of their surnames to form "Rigazzi's." They split amicably in 1961, and Louis Aiazzi took over the business. Joan Aiazzi died in March 2023 and was the widow of Louis Aiazzi's son.

Shaw's Coffee

Rigazzi's trademark is its frozen fish bowl beer schooner. I remember drinking root beer from a smaller schooner at Rigazzi's when my dad brought us there in the 1960s, while Aiazzi remembers drinking from a root beer fishbowl at Rigazzi's in the 1970s. "As a kid, there was nothing like it," she said. Fish bowls continue to abound at this popular eatery, but they usually contain beer.

I left Rigazzi's I made my way out of the neighborhood heading east on Shaw. I crossed South Kingshighway Boulevard and observed a traffic island with an old and time-honored bar in the middle: O'Connell's Pub. Founded in Gaslight Square in

1962, the pub moved to its present location in 1972. O'Connell's is known for straightforward bar fare, including stellar cheeseburgers.

Walking east on Shaw, I passed a building dear to everybody at Reedy Press. A fire in 2017 destroyed our old warehouse along with all of our books. Thankfully, the Missouri Botanical Garden offered to let us use its Commerce Bank Education Center for temporary storage. The Garden's generosity helped Reedy bounce back with greater ease.

My stroll continued to Vandeventer and Shaw. I had finished my journey through a place with myriad surnames that end in vowels. We Germans, whose names end with dissonant consonants, must listen with jealousy as the Italians introduce themselves.

Old Playground Pavilion
in Tower Grove Park

HENRY SHAW'S MASTERPIECE

Missouri Botanical Garden, Tower Grove Park, and Shaw Neighborhood

As close together as they could be, various knick-knacks and thingamabobs filled the sidewalk in front of Gringo Jones Imports at Shaw Boulevard and South Vandeventer Avenue. A fake sunflower. A Buddha. A statue of a dog. Outdoor furniture. If you've been there, you'll never forget it. Not seeing anything that interested me for purchase, I continued walking toward the Missouri Botanical Garden, following the iron fence that ran alongside me. It was a bright but slightly chilly afternoon on November 6. Birds chirped, and Halloween decorations lingered on houses, leftover pumpkins disintegrating on concrete steps.

Soon I reached the main entrance to the Missouri Botanical Garden, one of two signature contributions of an English immigrant named Henry Shaw (the other is Tower Grove Park). When I was a kid, people called the place Shaw's Garden. Shaw was born in Sheffield, England, in 1800 into a family that sold and made ironware. His father brought him to the United States on a business trip in 1818, and the next year, he returned here

View of Tower Grove House and gardens. Courtesy Don Korte

and threw himself into iron works, cutlery, and hardware that he sold to those settling in St. Louis or going west. By the end of the next two decades, Shaw was rich. He retired and focused on accumulating nearly 1,000 acres in the region, including one area where he would build a country home called Tower Grove House. The name referred to a large tower that proffered a view of a grove of sassafras and oak trees. He'd frequently visited the surrounding area, called the Prairie de Noyers or the Meadows of the Walnut Trees. He loved the prairie that extended west uncultivated by human hands. Instead, tall luxuriant grasses swayed in gentle breezes. He was about to cement a legacy that still enriches the lives of St. Louisans today.

In the 10 years or more after his retirement, Shaw made three trips through the US and Europe. After his last trip to Europe in 1851, Shaw decided to establish a great botanical garden for St. Louis based on two he had seen in England: Chatsworth and the Great London Exhibition.

In 1859, he officially opened his garden and then devoted his life to cultivating it (as well as Tower Grove Park and its surroundings). He incorporated input from German-born physician and botanist Dr. George Engelmann, who pointed out that European botanical gardens gave scientists a place to do their work. Engelmann convinced Shaw to collect botanical specimens and to add a library. The result is not only an attraction enjoyed by scores of people annually, but a place where education and important plant research happens.

While Shaw's vision and contributions enhance the city, his involvement in slavery tarnishes his legacy. When Shaw arrived in St. Louis, he wrote that America truly was a country of knavery, oppression, and slavery; however, he then went on to participate in this oppression. He first bought a slave in 1828, freed another in 1839, and had a bounty hunter track down four who had tried to escape in 1855. Records give the names of at least eight people total that he enslaved, although there are others whose names have been lost. On Juneteenth 2020, the Garden published the names of Shaw's known slaves, including Peach, Juliette, Bridgette, Joseph, Tabitha, Sarah, Jim, Esther, and Esther's children. Slavery is an indelible part of the history of the garden.

As it acknowledges Shaw's past, the Missouri Botanical Garden also promotes itself as a place for scientific research and public exploration. With more than 27,000 plants on permanent display, MBG is the nation's oldest continuously operating botanical garden. On any given day, you might find young couples, school groups, and families taking in the scenery. I'm partial to the Japanese Garden, but I also like getting

Courtesy Library of Congress

The Climatron at the Missouri Botanical Garden

lost among the shrubs of the maze. The dome called the Climatron can be a hotbox, but you'd expect that from a greenhouse that covers more than a half-acre. The complex structure features glass planes that consist of dozens of triangular shapes, and it houses a tropical environment that includes more than 1,000 plant species.

With the public tram tour, Shaw's original museum, children's garden, and other features, a decent tour can take all day, so I continued down Shaw toward Tower Grove Avenue. At the easternmost crossing of the intersection, a sign painted in brick announced the beginning of the Shaw neighborhood. I set my path southward toward Tower Grove Park. To my left, fences, homes, and dead-end streets limited access to the Shaw neighborhood. Administrative buildings for the Garden appeared at different points on both sides of the street; the ones on my right standing behind the imposing stone wall that runs along Garden property.

I eventually reached Magnolia Avenue and then crossed into Tower Grove Park, a 289-acre jewel Shaw donated to the city in 1868. It opened four years later and just celebrated its 150th anniversary in 2022. Until Forest Park opened to the public in 1876, Tower Grove Park was the biggest in the city. Take away the cars from the interior streets and Tower Grove Park looks pretty much the same as what Shaw originally designed.

I arrived at the circular drive in the middle of the park and photographed a statue of William Shakespeare facing east. On Saturday mornings and Tuesday afternoons in the spring, summer, and fall, the Tower Grove Farmers Market dominates the park. Located on the west side of a circle drive, the market used to attract about 5,000 people on a typical Saturday morning. Chris Geden, one of

Shakespeare statue
in Tower Grove Park

two market managers, said that more people likely come today, but it's hard to tell because people descend on the circle from all directions. According to market founders Patrick Horine and Jennifer Ryan, the market started in 2006 with 13 vendors. In 2020, more than 60 set up shop. All kinds of folks come to this family-friendly event, and they buy everything from produce to pastries to tamales to nonfood items like leather and jewelry. You can't beat the selection or the authenticity of this market.

Different areas of the park have different uses. Shaw had planned to build homes in certain spots, but no one bought them, said park Executive Director Bill Reininger. Many areas are fields used for softball, baseball, kickball, and other forms of recreation. The west end is more dedicated to nature. It features an elaborate stone entrance that faces Kingshighway, or "King's Highway," as it was called when Tower Grove Park was founded. Everything surrounding the entrance is made of stone, including a gatekeeper's house, two curving walls extending toward the street, and two 40-foot towers marking the entrance.

St. Louis author Amanda Doyle, author of *Tower Grove Park: Common Ground and Grateful Shade Since 1872*, notes that those who resided in the gatekeeper's house included Gus Fogt, the longtime head landscaper. He lived with his wife, daughter, and two sons at the house from 1959–1970. Plans call for the Missouri Department of Conservation to put an education headquarters/visitor welcome center in the building.

With that side trip finished, I headed east toward the other end of the park, which stretches from Kingshighway all the way to Grand Boulevard. The organization that runs the park uses a GPS system to keep track of the more than 300 kinds of trees that come from all over the world. Varieties include sycamores,

Piper Palm House

ash, elm, poplars, sweet gum, and scarlet oaks. When Shaw donated the park to the city, he stipulated that the land should always be a park and that the city must provide an appropriation each year for maintenance. He also required that an independent Board of Commissioners and staff should operate it. His choice of Victorian architecture adds to the park's character. The gates, pavilions, and park benches complement such buildings as the Piper Palm House, the Director's Residence, the Ruins, the Kingshighway Gatehouse, and the stables.

While heading east, I picked up Main Drive and passed waterlily and fountain ponds and a woodland pool to the left, near busts of classical composers. The park was active, as it is most days. I noticed a dog trying to keep up with a man riding a bicycle, avoiding the frame of a professional photographer's camera as they photographed a wedding party. On certain days, you'll encounter organized activities like the Festival of Nations or bike races. I enjoyed the relative quiet on a park bench with a news article from the day's Washington Post.

After a few minutes, I pocketed the phone and started north through a field to Magnolia Avenue. I eventually made my way toward 39th Street and exited the park. After walking north for about six blocks, I walked by Ices Plain and Fancy. Ices serves nitro ice creams flash-churned at 321 degrees below zero. A

neighborhood place, the ice cream parlor gets support from local families like the Gerstners, who are loyal customers. Jenny Gerstner, former president and current office manager of the Shaw Neighborhood Improvement Association grew up in a lovely home on Russell Boulevard. After she got married, she and her husband Jerrod bought the house from her parents, John and Terri Merideth, who live next door. Her sister and brother-in-law, Julia and Brad Burgess, live with their three kids on the same block.

Jenny talked about growing up in the neighborhood in the 1980s and attending St. Margaret of Scotland School. She remembers walking to school. But not all of her memories are pleasant. She recalls kids from her class talking about prostitutes hanging out near the school building. One neighborhood street that benefited from the neighborhood's revival is Flora Place. Developed in the mid-19th century by Henry Shaw as part of his residential influence on the neighborhood, the street runs east to west north of St. Margaret of Scotland Church. The high-end dwellings on Flora Place once housed some of the wealthiest St. Louisans and features architectural styles like Georgian, Tudor Revival, and Mission. At the northeast end of the Shaw Neighborhood is Shaw Place, a duplication of the area where Shaw grew up in England, featuring 10 brick Victorian homes.

But I didn't make it that far north. Instead, I turned east on Russell and crossed Grand, where my contemplation of Henry Shaw's importance to the South Side ended. He certainly left a mark.

Compton Hill Reservoir

MANSIONS AND A TOWN OF STRING

Compton Avenue and Virginia Avenue From I-44 to Bellerive Park

Back when I was a reporter, I could easily climb the 198 steps to the top of the Compton Hill Water Tower. Today, at 72, I'm not sure whether I could make it to the top of the 179-foot-high edifice at Compton Hill Reservoir Park. Even with seven landings where you can rest, the climb is tiring. But I remember how breathtaking it was to arrive at the top and look over the city through one of the windows.

Today though, I feel content to admire the structure from the bottom. The tower is now mostly ornamental, but it once—along with two other towers in the city—took in surges that occurred when pumps sent river water to the reservoir with high velocity. The standpipe inside the tower let the water travel upward, which neutralized the pressure and prevented geyser-like eruptions.

The tower is open regularly during warmer months and for special events, so it was open as I walked by. Visitors to the tower find it hard to miss the nearby *Naked Truth* statue honoring the work of three local German journalists. When it was dedicated in

1914, many were offended, including beer baron Adolphus Busch, because the woman portrayed was, well, naked.

Had I walked east on Russell, I could have taken a closer look at two fabulous old residences: the Fleur-de-Lys Mansion and the Magic Chef Mansion. Built in the 19th century, the Fleur-de-Lys Mansion now is a hotel. The Magic Chef Mansion went up in 1908 as the home of the founder of the Quick Meal & Magic Chef Stove Company.

Instead of using Russell, I took Longfellow Boulevard to continue my walk from the Shaw neighborhood. The path led me to a world reminiscent of scenes from the movie *Meet Me in St. Louis*. Close by, a small, inviting park splits Longfellow into two streets, the other being Hawthorne Boulevard. Pristine, turn-of-the-century

mansions face the park from both streets. The feel of the setting is exclusive, but Compton Heights (a name that the St. Louis Streets Index traces to the English Duke of Devonshire's Compton Place) is open to anyone, including drivers cutting through the neighborhood along with walkers and joggers. Throughout the year, the Compton Heights neighborhood hosts activities like horse-drawn carriage rides at Halloween, Weedless Wednesday garden parties, and a Christmas stroll with Santa Claus.

The Compton Heights neighborhood was developed at the pinnacle of the Gilded Age as a place for the city's elite.

Members of the city's German moneyed class and executives of such St. Louis behemoths as Anheuser-Busch lived in the neighborhood's brick and stone mansions.

Civil engineer Julius Pitzman laid out the neighborhood in 1888. Deed restrictions written in 1893 specified that all homes should stand the same distance from the street; they also required all homes to be single family and to be purchased at a then-huge minimum of $5,000 to $8,000 per house. Though the house designs all followed these rules, the architectural styles vary widely and include Romanesque, Colonial, Georgian, German Renaissance, Tudor, and Arts and Crafts. Turrets, dormers, hipped roofs, and terra cotta ornamentation all add to the charm and individuality of the neighborhood's homes. The Gay Nineties elegance remains, even if today's residents aren't as wealthy.

View from Grand Avenue in Compton Heights in 1890. Courtesy Missouri Historical Society, St. Louis

Today, Compton Heights is surrounded by Interstate 44, Grand Boulevard, Nebraska Avenue, and the backs of homes behind Shenandoah Avenue. At Shenandoah, I passed into Tower Grove East, a neighborhood on the upswing. From World War II to the 1980s and 1990s, the area struggled with decline, but urban rehabbers with vision have brought it back. Local government helped the process, but it was individuals who led the way.

It was in this bit of urban beauty, at Magnolia Avenue and South Compton, that I stopped for the day. I returned to that location in the afternoon on a cold November 13 and noticed a different kind of traffic-control device. Before me were 14 white concrete balls at the four corners of Magnolia and South Compton Avenues, ready to slow speeders as effectively as any speed bump. Altogether, six street corners on South Compton Avenue from Park Avenue to Arsenal Street have these concrete fixtures to slow down traffic. I stopped counting and kept moving to keep myself warm. It was 37 degrees, after all.

Roosevelt High School in 1939.
Courtesy Missouri Historical Society, St. Louis

Ahead was Roosevelt High School, which I passed during my walk following the footsteps of Ulysses Grant. Passing Roosevelt this time around, I paid particular attention to the four domes in the middle of the roof. That day, they reminded me of big green scoops of ice cream.

I continued south on Compton Avenue, crossed Gravois, and walked through part of the Benton Park West neighborhood. After a few blocks, I saw Gravois Park, which meant I was entering the Gravois Park neighborhood. The park was dedicated to Louis "Uncle Louie" Buckowitz in 1995. He died in 1999 at the age of 92 and was remembered as a former alderman and Democratic city leader who served the public for more than 60 years. As director of the city's Parks, Recreation, and Forestry Department, Uncle Louie organized Easter egg hunts at three city parks, including Gravois Park.

My stint in this smallish neighborhood ended once I reached Chippewa Street and the Dutchtown neighborhood. Many consider Dutchtown emblematic of the South City, filled with working class people, old brick homes, and pioneers of restoration.

At Compton and Meramec Street, I was reminded of what an imposing church can do to a street's appearance. At the high point of Meramec Street from South Grand Boulevard to South Broadway, St. Anthony of Padua Catholic Church stands out for its beauty and magnificence. The parish was founded in the 1860s for German-speaking farmers in Dutchtown, and the Franciscan Friars provided priests. Consecrated in 1869, their permanent Gothic-style church building seats 700, and the friars of the Sacred Heart Province continue to lead the parish.

Quaint storefronts surrounding St. Anthony's include Winkelmann Sons Drug, Urban Eats Cafe, and Behrmann's Tavern. Just south of Meramec on Virginia Avenue is Callisto Comics and Stories. Dave Smith runs the store in a freestanding brick building about the size of a studio apartment. It may be tiny, but Smith has filled it to the brim with books that celebrate the Avengers, the Masters of Kung Foo, Spider Man, and bunches of others. Dave got turned on to comics as a kid, enticed by the adventures and illustrations. He started selling online at first before eventually renting a store. He wanted a charmer in a standalone building that fit his budget, so it took a while. The variety of

St. Anthony of Padua

people in the neighborhood, as well as the consistent foot traffic, has helped business, which attracts customers from different parts of the metro.

Had I stuck to my original plan, I would have turned right at Compton and Meramec, but I didn't. Instead, I kept walking down Compton for a block that seemed like a canyon, where the houses stood on hills that sloped downward toward the street. That block ended at Osceola Street, where I noticed the Original Crusoe's, a longtime chicken and comfort-food establishment. South City still boasts a number of throwback eateries like Crusoe's. Taking Osceola west and then Virginia Avenue south brought me to the Stork Inn, a three-sided former restaurant and tavern built by beer baron August Busch himself. The two-and-a-half story Tudor Revival building stands on an island surrounded by Virginia, Taft, and Idaho Avenues. The building is covered with green brick on the outside and stucco and timber on the inside, matching the look of an inn in Bavaria. Built in 1910, the Stork Inn was the first of several businesses Busch founded pre-Prohibition to show that alcohol could be part of a respectable family activity like dining out. The tavern closed during Prohibition but reopened afterwards in 1933. The place closed for good in the 1990s and later was converted to an office by local architect Anthony Duncan.

When I met with Duncan, he told me the area was once called

Stork Inn.
Courtesy Jim Merkel

Shay's Donuts

Stringtown. It's been a while since the name was used officially, because the St. Louis Streets Index stopped referring to Virginia Avenue between Meramec Street and Bates Street as Stringtown Road in 1883. In the 1900s, you could reach the area by bus, trolley, or on foot to visit its numerous stores. I counted at least three dozen storefronts on the former Stringtown Road, though more than half appeared vacant. Sadly, this is the case for many buildings in southeast St. Louis. As neighborhoods deteriorate, the merchants move out. Happily, Shay's, an old-time doughnut place southeast of the old Stork Inn, remains open, and elsewhere along Compton and Virginia, churches occupy some storefronts.

About five blocks south of the old Stork Inn stands another three-sided edifice: the former Virginia Theater. August Busch built the theater on a skinny wedge formed by Virginia, Vermont Avenue, and Walsh Street at a cost of $40,000. A crowd of about 800 watched its first vaudeville show on December 11, 1910. It's hard to tell whether any of the original performers made it big, but a newspaper article noted how much excitement it stirred. A 1998 article about the Virginia Theater in the *South Side Journal* quoted old-timers raving about vaudeville nights and noting that movies changed as often as three

Virginia Theater in 1959. Courtesy Missouri Historical Society, St. Louis

Virginia Theater

times a week. Some recalled walking to matinees, where audience members could win bags of groceries and other prizes.

Run for much of its life by the Wehrenberg Theatres, the Virginia Theater closed in 1956. From then until around 2012, the public used it for plays, auctions, church services, and resale events. The city's Land Reutilization Authority now owns the building, which sits idle.

I decided to cross Walsh on the south side of the Virginia Theater and entered the Carondelet neighborhood. I neared Bates Street and turned left toward Bellerive Park. I walked by several storefronts. Most were vacant. I wondered if Virginia Avenue's best days were behind it. Hope returned, though, as I thought of some of the neighborhoods I've traversed on these walks. Maybe it was providential that I passed a resale store selling religious items inspired by Mary, Jesus, saints, angels. Those other places have managed to beat the odds with a dramatic comeback. Why not these very streets?

Stone row houses
on Steins Street

MY JAUNT THROUGH THE TOWN
OF EMPTY POCKETS

South Broadway from Bellerive Park to the River des Peres Greenway

South of the Gateway Arch, there's no better place to view the barges of the Mississippi River than Bellerive Park. This park off South Broadway at Bates Street offers a stunning view of the river, maybe better than the view downtown. The distractions are fewer, and the atmosphere is quieter.

I chose the park as my starting point for exploring Carondelet, a neighborhood that started as an early settlement. Founded in 1767, it was named after the Spanish governor of Louisiana but grew more slowly than its neighbor to the north. In 1870, St. Louis gobbled up Carondelet, which locals nicknamed Vide Poche, or empty pocket.

On that bright November afternoon, I started my walk by descending a stairway that brought me to Sister Marie Charles Park. The three-acre park sits on the banks of the Mississippi and floods when the river rises. Carondelet leaders named the park for Sister Marie Charles Buford, a Sisters of St. Joseph nun who spent three decades as executive director of the do-gooder group the

Carondelet Community Betterment Federation. She helped me many times when I covered South City after the year 2000. I always came away with news.

I headed south of the good nun's park and gazed at the buildings around us. South Broadway in Carondelet runs straight from Bellerive Park to where it passes over the River des Peres. Soon I was at street level passing mostly used car lots, brick, four-family flats, and factories with gigantic, rusting pipes connecting one to another. My view included a mammoth smokestack ascending to the sky and chain link fences, behind which sat tanker trucks in parking lots.

Eventually, I came to the first in a series of murals commissioned by local leaders with the support of the Regional Arts Commission. The first mural, by Ellie Balk, covers a warehouse with horizontal color blocks that vary in shape but seem to connect. Though Balk created the design and painted an outline, she encouraged community participation in the creation of the mural. On a Saturday in July 2017, St. Louis residents filled in Balk's outline with bright colors under her direction.

Farther down Broadway, I beheld a familiar set of painted eyes staring toward the street from the side of a structure on the property of Southern Metal Processing. Those signature eyes—stylized by artist Peat Wollaeger—appear in different places all over the St. Louis area. In this particular mural, Wollaeger used the metal ridges that extend from the building to create multiple viewing experiences. When approaching the eyes, they appear closed, but as the viewer gets closer, they begin to open.

Just west of Southern Metal Processing and uphill a few blocks, I glimpsed the St. Joseph of Carondelet Motherhouse. The place dates back to the arrival of two French nuns in Carondelet in 1836. The Sisters of St. Joseph quickly formed the first school in Carondelet as

Sisters of St. Joseph Motherhouse
Courtesy Missouri Historical Society, St. Louis

well as the first school for the deaf in the St. Louis area. Today, the complex on Minnesota Avenue hosts the local province along with most of the order's nuns in the United States. The Sisters of St. Joseph have provided secular and religious education for thousands of women and was the first home of Fontbonne University.

As I continued down Broadway, I arrived at the one-story brick storefront for the real estate office of Jaymes Dearing, a leader in the neighborhood. The side of his building displays another mural—an 1841 lithograph of the village of Carondelet. A couple of blocks south of Dearing's business is Loughborough Avenue, one of the few east-west streets that extends beyond Interstate 55 and reaches almost to the county line. From the end of World War II to the 1970s, Carondelet offered every kind of store. When I-55 came along, the highway offered people easy passage to county stores, including those in the South County Mall.

The decline in neighborhood commerce is apparent from the empty storefronts that line the west side of South Broadway. A sign extends overhead for L & S Broadway Café. I can easily imagine the activity that once took place inside—the sizzling of frying eggs, bacon, and hash browns at breakfast and the conversations of

customers over a table of Cokes, burgers, and crispy fries at lunch.

Carondelet might lack the charm of what you'll find in Lafayette Square, Soulard, and Shaw, where lovingly restored homes set the scene, but you won't find more historic housing anywhere else in the city. Stone row houses built by German immigrants survive on Steins Street, and some early French houses in the area might even date back to Carondelet's founding. Comparisons aside, I did come to appreciate the experience of walking this stretch of South Broadway. You get to see industry up close—factories, recyclers, warehouses, and other places where goods are made, processed, and stored.

You even encounter the occasional artisan, like David Moore, a custom furniture builder. Moore works with wood and metal and dabbles in 3D printing. He operates his business out of a renovated two-story building at Quincy and South Broadway. He formerly lived on the second floor with his family and likes to take bike rides on South Broadway, sometimes venturing to the motherhouse property to look out at the scrap yards and the river. Unfortunately, when I saw him, the pandemic had been keeping him from visiting the property.

Four blocks south of Moore's building, at Robert Avenue, the Carondelet neighborhood ends and the Patch neighborhood begins. The latter, which extends all the way to the River Des Peres, came about when the city decided on its current structure of 79 neighborhoods. Fred Hessel, executive director of the Carondelet Community Betterment Federation, considers the Patch still part of Carondelet, and his agency still serves the residents there.

Several establishments in the Patch attract people from outside the area, including the Off Track Saloon. A sign painted on the side of the building practically shouts the word, "Budweiser." West of Broadway, at 7900 Michigan Avenue, the Halfway Haus welcomes customers with food, drink, and music, while Stacked Burger Bar, at 7637 Ivory Avenue, serves an American favorite with style.

Another neighborhood standout is the Sinkhole, a rock 'n roll venue and recording studio that draws music lovers from all over town. Sinkhole owner Matt Stuttler spent his years after college playing in bands and booking clubs. In 2016, a friend approached him about opening a venue on South Broadway. He chose the current location because it was cheap and available for rent. He opened his doors, started booking bands, and reeled in customers. COVID-19 forced him to shut down for a time, but he remains committed to the neighborhood. He loves the old buildings and quirky stores like the Crystal Wizard Metaphysical Supply and the Belle-Aire Pawn Shop. He also enjoys the characters he encounters on South Broadway. He's heard talk that the street might develop into an entertainment district, but he isn't buying it, and neither is Hessel. Both men think Carondelet remains too isolated to attract meaningful business investment.

Sinkhole (left) and other South Broadway businesses

There is nowhere in Carondelet and Patch that offer basics that fill a cupboard and a refrigerator. A Dollar General provides some items, and the nearby South Public Market sells liquor, beer, and a few groceries. Residents with cars probably don't care, because they can drive across the interstate to Schnucks, but people without cars lack walkable options for shopping.

South Public Market was sufficient for my purposes that day. I bought a ginger ale and an ice cream bar and then enjoyed my cool refreshments at the edge of the parking lot. Facing the lot, a faded mural on the market building depicts a busy park scene, which includes a sailor and his family enjoying a picnic. The mural must refer to the South St. Louis Square Park, positioned on the other side of the lot and featuring the stone Anton Schmitt House, built in 1859. An informational sign near the house explains how James Eads did his part here to win the Civil War. Most St. Louisans know him for building the Eads Bridge after the war, but he also

designed ironclads, or steam-propelled warships, at shipyards in Carondelet that attacked Confederate positions on the Mississippi, the Ohio, and other rivers.

I spotted another mural across Broadway depicting a famous American trumpeter. Three hundred artists competed for this commission, but Ray Harvey won with his rendering of jazz notable Clark Terry, who lived in the area.

I finished my snack, continued along South Broadway and came across more houses. Two Queen Anne Victorian-style brick homes hint at the area's wealthy past. Closer to the River des Peres, the water becomes flood-prone. During the record-breaking 1993 flood, water covered the land there and almost caused a disaster at a Phillips Petroleum facility. As flood water invaded the property, pipes connected to propane tanks started floating. Had the water risen higher, propane might have escaped and set off explosions. The water receded before the worst happened, but many residents who lived close to the River des Peres suffered.

I thought of those residents as I crossed into the county, where Alabama Avenue becomes Lemay Ferry Road. My incursion into the county allows me to acknowledge Carondelet's gift to St. Louis County and the nation. In 1826, Carondelet sold 1,700 acres to the federal government for a military installation named for Thomas Jefferson. That purchase, for the outrageous price of $5, led to the construction of Jefferson Barracks. From that point, soldiers set out to protect the new land acquired in the Louisiana Purchase. Military notables like Robert E. Lee and Ulysses Grant were trained at the barracks, and much later, soldiers spent time there through the end of World War II.

Carondelet Park
Boathouse Lake

GRAFFITI, A LAKE, AND GRAVESTONES IN A PARK

Through Carondelet Park

O
n November 26, I headed for the Carondelet Connector. I started my northbound trek on the River des Peres Greenway at Alabama Avenue and Germania at 9 a.m. I went under the I-55 bridge over Germania, crossed Germania, and started walking the connector, a walkway that links the greenway to Carondelet Park. At the north end of the connector, a bridge carries Loughborough Avenue over a sidewalk and train tracks, which join with the same tracks I'd encountered on Morgan Ford near Arsenal and Chippewa Street. On a wall running opposite the tracks are multicolored strips of graffiti, painted white, light blue, red, black that almost resemble letters, many of which I didn't recognize. The art that adorned the wall closer to me was different. Amidst a generous portion of light blue was a rendering of a woman. I'm no art expert, but it looked kinda nice.

Anthony Duncan, an architect I spoke to about Compton and Virginia Avenues, contends that, despite what many would assume, graffiti artists stick to rules. Duncan, the owner of the

Carondelet Park Rec Complex

three-sided building that once housed the Stork Inn, said that buildings kept active by an owner rarely get hit, and only abandoned spaces bear the brunt.

I walked out from under the bridge and saw the Carondelet Park Recreation Complex to the right. Farther along stood a very tall tree with all its branches and bark missing. To its right were ample piles of mulch and wood chips yielded from dying trees by the city's forestry division. The city offers these remains for free at a handful of city parks including Carondelet.

In time, the winding trail delivered me to a crosswalk at Grand and Holly Hills Drives. I walked to my car and left for the day.

Six days later, shortly after 3 p.m. on December 2, I stood at the same crosswalk ready to finish the second half of my route. Multicolored leaves blanketed the ground. Walkers like me filled the trails, ready to discover all the glories of this pastoral gem. Carondelet Park was established in 1875.

As I observed different features of the park, I spotted a mansion in the southeast area of the park that once belonged to the Alexander Lacy Lyle family. Now owned by the city, the house is in bad shape, with windows broken and boarded up and raccoons taking up residence, but good times may

Lyle House. Courtesy Missouri Historical Society, St. Louis

CARONDELET PARK
→ Park Exit
→ Tennis Courts
← Lyle House
← Rec Complex
← Mulch/Compost Area

be ahead. A fundraiser was launched in 2021 to renovate the building and to determine a good use for it.

I headed away from the mansion on a wandering street and passed a lovely pavilion on my right. Soon I arrived at the Carondelet Park Boathouse Lake. The boathouse serves as a venue for large gatherings like family reunions and weddings, but the lake is the real draw. A photo taken nearly a century ago shows boats floating along the water. These days, you won't see boat traffic, but you'll find anglers on the banks hoping to attract the rainbow trout, bluegill, and white crappie stocked by the city's conservation department.

On that particular day, when temperatures ranged from the 50s to the low 70s, 20 or more people lingered at the lake with their poles. Some fished from docks in front of the boathouse, while others sought their prizes from the sidewalks that surround the water. Those anglers might have looked with interest at ducks swimming and quacking around in the water, but no one tried to catch them. Instead, a handful of ducks sat under a fountain, enjoying the water and seemingly unaware of the people around them. Their brethren seemed to be swimming happily elsewhere around the lake.

St. Louisans enjoying a day out on the lake in 1925.
Courtesy Missouri Historical Society, St. Louis

I returned to the park on a chilly afternoon and found the same number of people casting their lines. One was Vern Hellmann, who had been fishing at Boathouse Lake for about four years. Hellmann lives only about a mile away and I caught him during his first winter fishing outing for trout. Another angler, Dave Jones, also fishes there year-round, never keeping his catch. Meanwhile, Marion Bender, the third person I talked to, comes for a different kind of fishing: the trash in the lake, including branches and plastic bottles. She said she comes every day with a trash grabber to pull litter from the water. On the day I approached her, she was hard at work at the southeast corner.

I marched westward and soon was face to face with Horseshoe Lake, which was created in 1913 when workers combined nine sinkholes. When I walked farther out of the park, I found myself at the corner of Leona Street and Loughborough, back among the houses. Not far away, was a place I knew well; a couple of blocks north on Leona Street, my dad lived there with his second wife after my mother died. Rather than head down that path, I continued west on Loughborough and arrived at a collection of stores and businesses at Morgan Ford Road. A dentist's office. A smoke shop. Two auto repair shops. A Save A Lot grocery store.

The most interesting among them was Geoffrey J. Seitz's violin shop. Born in 1954, Seitz grew up in Lemay and started playing

old-time fiddle music in 1973 during his first year in college at the University of Missouri–St. Louis. In Spokane, Washington, he met a craftsman who taught him how to make and repair violins. He opened the storefront at 4171 Loughborough Avenue in 1987 and plies his trade six or seven days a week in a chaotic shop where violins seem to occupy every square inch. He makes and repairs violins, violas, and cellos using old techniques, preferring hand tools and horsehide glue over modern glues. He is a true craftsman, the kind my father appreciated. My dad, a piano craftsman, often took my family to shops like Seitz's. He loved talking to Seitz because they both made their living with musical instruments. The appreciation was mutual; Seitz said that the South Side has always been the place where you could get things made or fixed.

West of the violin shop, Loughborough descends a long hill. At the bottom, open land faces both sides of the street. The land on the south side of the street is part of Saints Peter & Paul Cemetery

Saints Peter & Paul Cemetery

while St. Marcus Commemorative Park, formerly the German Evangelical St. Marcus Cemetery before closing in 1960, occupies the north side (although some graves still remain). A little further back on Loughborough, I found a large traffic-signal control box. Painted eyes and mouths adorned both sides, likely meant to bring park visitors a smile. Since then, sad to say, someone defaced it beyond recognition.

Courtesy Jim Merkel

The Record Exchange

LITTLE GUYS HOLD THE LINE

Hampton Avenue from Loughborough Avenue to Arsenal Street

In other areas of South City, I was surrounded by century-old houses and parks with fountains, but the beginning of my walk through Hampton looked different. I began next to a gas station with a view of the Area 51 smoke shop, a store illuminated by green letters and filled with glass pipes, herbal supplies, electronic cigarettes, hookahs, and more. Nearby, a wheelchair lay unattended with various bags and pillows and a cardboard sign that read, "God bless homeless. Please help." The chair's inhabitant was not around, and my task that day, the afternoon of December 11, was to walk Loughborough and part of Hampton. It was only 4:10 p.m., and already the light was dimming.

After I crossed Gravois on Loughborough, I found a series of brick and stone houses with covered porches. On one side of the street were two-story houses and, on the other, narrow one-story homes. On the steps of one apartment building were pumpkins, even though Halloween had passed more than six weeks ago. Other lawns displayed Christmas decorations, one house sign announcing that "Jesus Is the Reason for the Season" and that we should keep all life sacred. On steps leading to another apartment building, a figurine of an angel proclaimed good tidings to everyone. Below her, three artificial reindeer stood ready for Santa's Christmas Eve journey.

Daylight was fading fast as I reached Hampton Avenue. However, once I crossed Hampton and hung a right, storefronts lit the way. Most of the stores were small shops managing to survive in an era dominated by big ones. Merchants on the same block included Smoke N Bones BBQ, Yapi Mediterranean Subs and Sandwiches, Karate Life Studio, and Southside Hardware. The karate studio was busy with kids learning self-defense, and at the hardware store, clerks who know their paint and screwdrivers, provided old-fashioned customer service not common in places like Lowes and Home Depot. Such is life on this throwback retail strip.

In many city neighborhoods, when local leaders try to revive an area, the solution involves attracting destinations like bars, restaurants, and entertainment venues. That's worked, especially

in the Grove, and Hampton offers plenty of food and drink options. But you'll also find stores for collectible toys, rare coins and currency, and shoe repairs to go along with more typical places like hair salons and insurance agencies.

All kinds of merchants have shingles up on Hampton, including Rhonda Young, aka the STL Balloon Lady, LLC. Young initially grew her balloon business out of her house, but eventually she got tired of seeing every square inch of her home taken up by balloon displays for clients. She decided to find a building and drove around the streets of St. Louis asking God to lead the way, when she found her current storefront for lease. The place is perfect for her, since Hampton is clean, easy to find, and doesn't have a lot of crime. Here, she creates at least 200 displays per year for occasions like weddings, corporate events, proms, birthday parties, homegoing celebrations, and other events.

Heading north on Hampton, restaurants, mostly independent, appeared on virtually every corner I passed. At the intersection of Hampton and Eichelberger, I encountered one of the more interesting places on my route. Occupying a two-story space once used as a library, the Record Exchange offers the best in used vinyl, CDs, and DVDs. Ever since Jean Haffner founded the business in the late 1970s, traditionalists have gravitated to the store. At a cluttered checkout counter, Jean said records were his passion growing up in the 1950s and 1960s. As an adult, he got tired of working 9 to 5, so he decided to do what he enjoyed—selling records. With the advent of the CD, many people dismissed vinyl as a dying format, but Haffner disagreed. CDs give a sampling sound, but records deliver the full sound. Records last forever, as long as you take care of them.

Just down the street is another longtime St. Louis establishment—Slyman Brothers and Sons Appliances. Now with four locations, Slyman was founded in 1965 and opened its store at 4900 Hampton in the mid-1980s, when current sales manager Bobby Slyman was only four. Small businesses often struggle to make it in appliances these days, but Bobby Slyman says his

Courtesy Jim Merkel

company succeeds by participating in a mass buying group to save on wholesale purchases of high-quality brands. The movement encouraging people to buy local has also helped their business, which comes largely from the surrounding neighborhoods. According to Bobby Slyman, the store also benefits from reaching out to the community and donating to local churches.

Throughout my walk on Hampton, I received regular reminders that Christmas was a mere two weeks away. In one instance, a Santa stood outside a store and offered holiday greetings to all who passed. In others, brightly lit trees greeted customers just inside the building. But in my view, the most impressive holiday decorations weren't meant as decorations at all. They came in the form of huge traffic control balls painted bright red. These inadvertently festive balls stood apart in even increments in front of Target at Hampton and Chippewa. How huge are they? You can spot them via satellite on Google Earth.

After I arrived at Chippewa Street and crossed Hampton, I turned off my tracker for the night. I resumed my walk a few days later at 4:03 pm at the Hampton McDonald's and crossed Chippewa. As I walked farther, I noticed the building styles changing around me. North of Chippewa, the buildings on Hampton vary in size, shape, and style. The Lindell Bank on the northwest corner

Statue at Lindell Bank.
Courtesy Jim Merkel

of Hampton and Chippewa has a marble exterior fronted by two sculptures by Richard H. Ellis of Grants Pass, Oregon. One shows a mother and child above two swans, and the other depicts a father, a son, and a fawn. You don't expect a place that keeps track of money to show artistic sensibilities.

Farther to the north is Chick-fil-A, one of many fast-food restaurants with drive-throughs that line Hampton from Loughborough to Arsenal. Outside Chick-fil-A, cars queue up for chicken sandwiches like cattle lining up for feed. What a business!

In a matter of minutes, I reached the 27-acre Tilles Park. The park's well-known premises feature a roller hockey rink, tennis and pickleball courts, softball and baseball fields, and relatively new basketball courts. But if you show up during the holidays to see the annual Winter Wonderland lights display, you'll be disappointed. That display appears at the other Tilles Park, at Litzinger and McKnight Roads in St. Louis County. Both parks exist because of the generosity of businessman Andrew "Cap" Tilles, who donated his St. Louis County farm in 1932 to the city as a place for kids from the county and city to play. Tilles lost both of his parents at a young age and made the parks in memory of his mother, Rosalie Tilles. Then in 1957, St. Louis County bought the 59-acre park from the City of St. Louis for $429,000. The City used that money to buy and develop its own Tilles Park at Fyler and Hampton. The gift of Andrew "Cap" Tilles had yielded two parks for the region.

Rosalie's Garden in Tilles Park

Just north of the park across Fyler Avenue is the Hampton Gardens apartment complex. Once, it was a potter's field for St. Louis, but in 1950, the city leased those 32 acres for $100 a year to a company that built hundreds of apartment units there. The city also agreed to waive property taxes and taxes on any development. Many observers complained that the city should have requested more bids, while others said the apartments would attract the wrong crowd. Mayor Joseph Darst argued the city would get more than $100,000 in taxes through the project and claimed the project would transform an unsightly parcel into a model community for 500 families. He won, and the city signed an agreement for 75 years ending in 2025. Then in 2020, the city approved a new, 50-year lease with a sharp increase that raised the annual payment to $165,000. Under the new terms, that amount will jump to $209,000 by 2070 but includes an option to buy the property in 2050. Sounds like a fair deal to me but what do I know?

As I continued down Hampton, I passed blocks of nothing but houses on a busy city street. Finally, I reached the end of my walk for the day: Arsenal Street and Hampton. On the southwest side is Ari's Restaurant & Bar, a popular place if you like Greek food and high-quality breakfast buffets. I love being anywhere I can say, "It's all Greek to me." At the northwest side is a nail salon that was once a Velvet Freeze ice cream parlor. Decades ago, Velvet Freeze had locations throughout the city, the county—everywhere people liked cold treats. Those of us who spent our early years slurping down Velvet Freeze chocolate malts will never forget that wonderful taste.

Sublette Park

THE END OF THE ROAD

Arsenal Street from Hampton Avenue to Kingshighway Boulevard, then North to I-64

I n a car, you'd miss it. But walking, you feel it. At the bottom of St. Louis, when I crossed the River des Peres from Carondelet, I was about 415 feet above sea level. At Hampton Avenue and Arsenal Street on December 20, 2021, I was about 200 feet higher. We're not talking mountains, but 200 feet is still a drag to climb. A short walk on the north side of Arsenal Street brought me to Sublette Park, where a hill reaches 614 feet, the highest point in the city. In 1872, the Social Evil Hospital was built to treat prostitutes with sexually transmitted diseases. After the building was razed around 1914, the surrounding land became the park named after the fur traders William and Solomon Sublette.

I walked along Arsenal opposite the park, where newer frame houses lined the street. Some of these houses stand on the property of the bygone Harry S. Truman Restorative Center, the last city facility that directly provided healthcare service to the public. Among other places, that system once included the City Hospital and the Homer G. Phillips Hospital. The center closed in 2004 because of high costs and low use.

The St. Louis Forensic Treatment Center South as it appeared in 1870. Courtesy Missouri Historical Society, St. Louis

The site itself had an unpleasant history. The St. Louis Chronic Hospital for the elderly opened on the property in 1871 and provided inadequate care for decades. It filled with older people who couldn't get into the overcrowded state hospital just blocks east. And prior to 1871, the St. Louis County Farm, or Poor House, occupied the property. It operated as an isolation hospital, a nursing home, and a place for indigent patients.

But when people think of this stretch of Arsenal, the state hospital most likely comes to mind. I spotted the imposing brick building on the right as I approached Macklind and then got a more open view after passing Fire House Engine Number 35.

The main domed building towers over South City. Originally called the St. Louis County Lunatic Asylum, it's now the St. Louis Forensic Treatment Center South. It serves people who can't be prosecuted because of mental illness.

The doctors and nurses who worked at the facility in the early days may have been passionate, but some of their treatments caused more harm than good. They injected patients with strong drugs that failed to help, and in some cases performed lobotomies that left patients incapacitated. As with the treatment of many illnesses, mental health treatments improved over time and so did the facility.

According to a staff member, the asylum held 130 patients in 1869 and by 1970 had grown to 3,000. That number dropped sharply as officials worked to integrate patients into the greater community. Today, the center treats about 180 patients in buildings on the east and west sides of the main building, which is now used for administration and storage.

I confess a personal interest in the place. In 1871, for reasons I'll probably never know, my great-great grandmother Anna Merkel was admitted to the asylum. She was transferred to a poor house in 1878, and in 1885, a city health official reported that she was a hopeless lunatic. That information came from Charles Francis of the city health department, in an interview with a local newspaper. Forget that details of anybody held in an institution for the mentally ill never would be released today. The comments tell bunches about the times and my family.

The occasion was an effort by one of Anna's sons to tidy up the estate of her husband Louis C. Merkel, who recently had died. Charles Merkel petitioned to represent his youngest brother, 17-year-old Emil, because their mother (Anna) was incompetent to manage the estate. "If the son has an estate, she must have an estate also, and she should not be in the Poor House. Her friends ought to take her away and place her in a private asylum," Francis told the *St. Louis Globe-Democrat*. "It is an imposition on the city to keep her in the Poor House, and I have no doubt the health commissioner will immediately notify the woman's friends that they will have to provide for her." In the 19th century, misbehaving wives were known to be committed to the asylums by their husbands. Nobody knows, and any

suspicion may be unfair to the husband. The truth is nobody knows what happened from then until Anna died in 1909. But I doubt she improved. It seems crass to treat her case merely as a matter of taxpayer savings, but it also seems clear that my family could have done more to ease the sufferings of Anna Merkel. To consider the torment of a real mental health patient in the 1870s and 1880s who shares one's DNA brings the pain of all of them to life. As for myself, I will bless the memory of anyone who lifted a finger to ease the hurt of Anna Merkel.

Thoughts of Anna disappeared as I left the facility. Walking away from it to the east, I noticed the elevation decreasing. A bridge brought me over a rail line. To my left was a Schnucks, and a little while to my right was the old Southwest High School building that opened in 1936 at Kingshighway Boulevard and Arsenal Street. Today, parts of the building are used as the campuses of two magnet schools, the Central Visual and Performing Arts High School and the Collegiate School of Medicine and Bioscience, an intensive school meant to lead to careers in various works of healing.

On October 24, 2022, the schools suffered through a school shooting that took the lives of a student and a teacher at Central Visual. While students and staff members barricaded themselves in classrooms, police entered the building and exchanged fire with the gunman, who was eventually struck and killed. Dead were a 15-year-old student, Alexandria Bell; and physical education teacher, Jean Kuczka, 61. Six students were wounded. The event devastated the school

community and its neighbors, who extended their condolences and support in the aftermath. Students waived pictures of the two victims when they returned to class on January 17. Extra security and counseling was made available on that day, and a campaign was underway to raise money for students' college expenses. Five artists painted murals on lockers in school hallways. Frequent incidents of shooting violence around the country may numb us, but they come alive when they happen where you drive every day.

As I crossed Kingshighway the day of my walk, I thought about how great it was that these schools sought to meet the interests and talents of its students. Arriving at the west side of Tower Grove Park, I kept my eye on the other side of the street and passed a series of attractive homes along with the Journey Church Tower Grove at Odell Street and Kingshighway. Holy Innocents Catholic Church occupied the building until it closed in 2005.

When I reached the park's stone entrance at Magnolia Avenue and Kingshighway, I tapped a foot on Magnolia to signify the end of the day's hike. I resumed my route late in the afternoon the day after Christmas. The years have brought changes to many areas of South City, both good and bad. But the changes to South Kingshighway from Arsenal to Interstate 64 make it a boulevard in the best sense. Two rebuilt railroad bridges offer expansive views of the city to the east and west. Today's atmosphere was just right. The sky was darkening and a fog had settled in, giving the area a mysterious look.

Before I reached the first bridge, I arrived at the site of a real life, made-for-the-movies bank robbery at Southwest Avenue. The attempted heist at Southwest Bank on April 24, 1953, had everything—

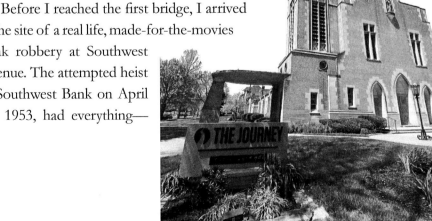

Fred W. Bowerman. Public domain

so much that it inspired a Steve McQueen movie filmed on site in 1958. The four would-be bandits expected to be in and out quickly, but their plans went awry. The leader of the attempted heist, Fred W. Bowerman, was shot after he took a hostage. He later died from his wounds, and his partners in crime didn't fare much better. To avoid being sent back to prison, one robber shot himself and another surrendered after police wounded him in a gun battle. The getaway driver fled the scene and was later apprehended in Chicago.

The Great St. Louis Bank Robbery made for a gripping story even if the robbery itself wasn't so great, but development threatens the story's setting. Part of the old Southwest Bank property has been turned into a Walgreens. Always a Walgreens. However, the section where the attempted heist occurred—now BMO Harris Bank—remains.

Walking past the bank, I continued uphill on the first railroad bridge. Below me was the track of the Union Pacific Railroad's line through South City that I'd passed on Arsenal. On the other side of the bridge was Interstate 44. Next to the eastbound exit to Kingshighway, a man held a piece of cardboard with a message asking for assistance. That particular exit gets a lot of traffic. For the same reason, you'll often see people asking for money near the westbound entrance to I-44.

Believe it or not, just a block north at U-Haul Moving & Storage, you can stop in and view significant architectural work—the drop ceiling on the first-floor lobby. Architect

BMO Harris Bank

The Hill

82°

Isamu Noguchi designed the lobby in the mid-century modern building when it housed American Stove-Company's Magic Chef, which manufactured appliances nearby on The Hill. U-Haul bought the building and covered the ceiling in the 1990s, but in 2016, heeding appeals by preservationists, the company uncovered and restored the ceiling, meant to resemble a sculpted landscape.

Past U-Haul and McRee Avenue, a second bridge took me over more railroad tracks. Antique street lights illuminated my path. To the northeast, a crane near the BJC campus looked downright festive with its red lights. Another medical building going up, or so I surmised. At Manchester, a sign over the street announced the western entrance to the Grove. I walked three blocks to the dead end of Chouteau Avenue, next to the old expressway, and ended my walk for the day.

I returned to that spot shortly after 4 p.m. on New Year's Eve with my wife, Lorraine, and my brother, Charles, whom I asked to photograph the completion of my last walk. While he snapped pictures of me, a happy guy with a white beard and a fedora passed us and let me know that I "wasn't that cute." "You're right," I said. "I'm downright ugly."

The three of us crossed the pedestrian bridge over Interstate 64 and looked out at the roaring traffic below. About halfway across, I figured I had crossed the invisible line between South City and the Central Corridor. My walk was complete. We strolled to the north side of the bridge even though the journey was over, enjoying the last bits of sunlight of the year. I'd completed all my walks by the tail end of 2021. More than a year of writing, editing, proofing, and printing would follow. Nonetheless, with my wife and brother nearby, it was good to think that one year's work was over. I'd seen the place I love in ways I've never seen it before.

EPILOGUE

Randy Vines, co-owner of the STL Style House, says that what he loves the most about South City is that the people are as real as they come. "There is no pretense, just a real sense of history, authenticity, and a distinct urban culture," he says. Jeff and his brother Randy spend their days celebrating St. Louis with their merchandise. He calls South City a living museum. Most neighborhoods were built up around busy streetcar lines, before the automobile became the preferred mode of transportation, he said. "That makes them more walkable, accessible, and conducive to human interaction."

Working on this book, I must have spoken to dozens who agree. They say they would rather live here than anywhere else. Through all my research for this book, I continue to find that South City offers its residents a warm, comfortable sense of being home, and many longtime Southsiders would feel lost elsewhere. But what is the meaning of this place? And what makes someone a Southsider besides their address?

Areas like ours have sweet routines repeated through the years, like my neighbor Harry's morning ritual. Harry lived a few porches down from my house and would sit on a weather-proof couch every day, drinking coffee early in the morning. It might be January or July; the only difference was how he dressed. As a retiree, he had the time—plus, his wife Dot had banned him from smoking inside. He and Dot, who always sat in a chair next to him, would gossip, talking about fishing or going on the vacation they never took. Sometimes they were joined by their son Clayton, another neighbor, Don, or by my wife and I. Unfortunately, Harry died of cancer, and Don followed him soon after. But to this day, Dot calls friends or reads while sitting on that weather-proof couch. Sometimes, we stop by, in part, to continue this South City ritual.

Gathering on porches, lawns, and driveways is how people in my part of the city socialize. Every Friday, a homeowner in Lindenwood Park invites the neighbors to gather on his driveway and relax. People bring drinks and sometimes food for the crowd. A video of a Cardinals game is projected on the house next door.

Southsiders like to keep things informal and welcoming. Everyone belongs, regardless of their walk of life. Firefighters live next to doctors who live next to teachers who live next to stockbrokers who live next to tuck pointers and lowly journalists like me. The social dynamics may have evolved from neighborhoods being walkable and houses being close together. I doubt anyone could find these dynamics elsewhere.

Any person who moves to South City is greeted by our special brand of community. Ray Oldenburg described that homeward feeling in his 1989 book *The Great Good Place: Cafes, Coffee Shops, Bookstores, Bars, Hair Salons, and Other Hangouts at the Heart of the Community*. Oldenburg highlights the need for free and informal spaces for people to connect, for people to feel at home, where everything is right. The South Side does this naturally.

In South City, parks are the purest examples of Oldenburg's free and informal public spaces. They come in many sizes and shapes, but all provide opportunities for people to interact and relax. Other spaces that offer the same include block parties, parish festivals, and farmers markets like Tower Grove and Soulard. One fall Sunday, Lorraine and I attended the birthday party of a friend near the Rockwell Beer Garden at Francis Park. Grownups imbibed and chatted while kids ran around and played. I'm not sure how many would have come to that spot on a weekend afternoon if someone hadn't installed an outdoor patio and concession stand in what used to be a parks maintenance building.

I gained a full appreciation of South City's affinity for gatherings on a Saturday early in October 2022. I was driving through several neighborhoods to determine photo subjects for this book and found people congregating everywhere. On The Hill, the annual Italian Heritage Parade was about to begin. I spotted Joe Vollmer, owner of Milo's Bocce Garden and ward alderman, looking electric in a Hawaiian shirt. After snapping some photos, I hopped in my car and headed to the Grove, where revelers celebrated Oktoberfest over pints and German music. But that wasn't the only Oktoberfest taking place in South City that day. I also discovered one happening several neighborhoods away in Soulard outside the market building. The celebrations were the same but different, just like each South City neighborhood. The mansions of Compton Heights look nothing like the two-story brick houses of Dutchtown or the frame houses of Bevo Mill. However, these neighborhoods all have a "main street," where businesses and organizations line for several blocks. Cherokee Street serves as the main street for the adjacent Benton Park West and Gravois Park neighborhoods; Manchester Avenue for Forest Park Southeast; and Marconi Avenue for The Hill. The revitalization of Southampton's business artery, Macklind Avenue, has lifted the neighborhood to new heights. I learned that when the main street bustles with activity, people will come.

What else did I learn from walking 45 miles of South City?

- The Hill's heritage of Italian immigrants from the Lombardy region of northern Italy and from Sicily in the south has resulted in restaurants that serve the best cuisine from both groups.

- In St. Louis Hills, the bold vision of a brilliant developer yielded a rich mix of dwellings—many with singular character—on the southwestern edge of St. Louis. He didn't add businesses, but if you want proof that small merchants are alive and well in South City, walk the 2.5

miles of Hampton Avenue from Loughborough Avenue to Arsenal Street. You'll pass the big dogs like Target, McDonald's, and Chick-fil-A, but you'll discover more thriving independent businesses.

- The restored neighborhoods in South City provide zest and remind a person of a cocktail made with perfectly aged whiskey. The blend includes rare establishments like John D. McGurk's Irish Pub and Garden, South Broadway Athletic Club, and the Soulard Farmers Market. Meanwhile, Lafayette Square is an elegant wine you'd seek at SqWires Restaurant. Its 19-century palatial homes testify to what can happen when urban restorationists dedicate themselves to returning a property to its original glory.

- And some day, Dutchtown may again be reminiscent of the Budweiser on draft you'd consume at Behrmann's Tavern. This working-class neighborhood is distressed in different spots, but its down-to-earth charm and classic brick homes and storefronts—especially near Meramec and Virginia—could inspire a comeback.

Rough edges may be rare in the suburbs, but there's nothing like the energy and excitement generated by the colorful and eclectic neighborhoods of South City. Here, we can feel history reverberating around us. Personality abounds in the people, the buildings, and in the streets themselves. Walking South City is like digging into a wild salad with a wide variety of ingredients—lettuce, onions, deli meat, garlic powder, black pepper, balsamic vinaigrette, and your pick of dressing. Everything is different. Everything belongs. Everybody's welcome. If you don't believe me, or if you're just curious, come visit and take a walk.

SOURCES

Preface

Bryson, Bill, *A Walk in the Woods: Rediscovering America on the Appalachian Trail* (New York: Broadway Books 1998).

Lafayette Park Conservancy, The Thomas Hart Benton Conservancy, https://www.lafayettepark.org/project/the-benton-monument/

McClellan, Bill, *Fine local authors get some publicity*. Stltoday, December 10, 2010, Accessed September 24, 2022.

Prologue

Archdiocese of St. Louis, History, https://www.archstl.org/history/, Accessed: September 11, 2022.

Hammonds Books, https://hammondsbooks.net/, Accessed October 5, 2022.

Merkel, Jim, *Hoosiers and Scrubby Dutch*, First Edition, St. Louis, Reedy Press, 2010.

Naffziger, Chris, interview.

Naffziger, Chris, A closer look at sinkholes and former quarries in St. Louis. https://www.stlmag.com/history/sinkholes-in-st-louis/, Accessed Sept. 7, 2022.

Nineteen Ninety and 2020 St. Louis Data Results, in City of St. Louis web site, https://www.stlouis-mo.gov/

Great Rivers Greenway Mission-Vision, https://greatriversgreenway.org/mission-vision/, Accessed September 13, 2022.

Hurley, Stephen D. interview.

Patterson, Steve, interview.

Sells, George, email to author, September 21, 2022.

St. Louis Street Tree Information, https://www.stlouis-mo.gov/government/departments/parks/forestry/documents/upload/Street-Tree-Information1.pdf, Accessed September 9, 2022.

Railroad Map of St. Louis, https://dl.mospace.umsystem.edu/umsl/islandora/object/umsl:200439, Accessed September 13, 2022.

Washington University in St. Louis, William H. Danforth, https://wustl.edu/about/history-traditions/chancellors/danforth/, Accessed September 13, 2022.

On the Path of Ulysses Grant

Age of the USA Presidents, https://presidenstory.com/stat_age.php, February 4, 2022.

Affton, Missouri - History - The 19th Century - Gravois Road, https://www.afftonchamber.com/history-of-affton.html

Beaux Arts Banks, Jefferson and Gravois, http://stlouispatina.com/beaux-arts-bank-jefferson-and-gravois/

Chouteau, Auguste, American Fur Trader, Encyclopedia Britannica, https://www.liquisearch.com/affton_missouri/history/the_19th_century/gravois_road, Accessed March 3, 2021.

Chouteau, Auguste, https://www.britannica.com/biography/Auguste-Chouteau

Early Beginnings in St. Louis, http://www.museum.state.il.us/RiverWeb/landings/Ambot/SOCIETY/SOC5.htm, Accessed March 2, 2021.

Exclusive recipe, https://www.feastmagazine.com/recipes/article_65af773e-c916-11e0-8b2d-0019bb30f31a.html

Greater Gravois Initiative, https://nextstl.com/2015/11/greater-gravois-initiative-produces-vision-for-a-better-gravois-awaits-modot-plan

Gravois Avenue from Tucker Boulevard to west of Grand Boulevard, https://en-us.topographic-map.com/maps/kfp/St-Louis/

http://www.museum.state.il.us/RiverWeb/landings/Ambot/SOCIETY/SOC5.htm, Accessed March 2, 2021.

The History of Saint Louis Public School's Theodore Roosevelt High School, https://www.slps.org/domain/5317, Accessed August 20, 2021.

https://www.liquisearch.com/affton_missouri/history/the_19th_century/gravois_road. Accessed March 19, 2021 and other times.

Institute of Christ the King, https://institute-christ-king.org/stlouis-home

Kutis, Thomas III, interviews, February 19, 2021 and other dates.

Sacco, Nick, park ranger, Ulysses S. Grant National Historic Site, emails to author, January 25 and 26.

Merkel, Jim Hoosiers and Scrubby Dutch Second Edition (St. Louis: Reedy Press, 2014).

National Park Service website, https://www.nps.gov/ulsg/index.htm

The Route 66.com, https://www.theroute-66.com/saint-louis.html

St. Michael the Archangel Orthodox Church, https://stmichaelstlouis.org/

What is Tudor Architecture? https://www.thespruce.com/tudor-architecture-4788228, Accessed March 19, 2021.

St. Louis Public Schools, October 29, 1922, November 25, 1922.

A Ride on Route 66

Elz, Ron (Johnny Rabbitt), interview, March 4, 2021, and other dates, and factsheet he provided.

Gravenhorst, Edna Famous-Barr: St. Louis Shopping at its Finest (Charleston, S.C. The History Press, 2014).

J.C. Penney closing Hampton Village store in St. Louis, holding liquidation sale. Dec. 21, 2017. https://www.stltoday.com/business/local/jcpenney-closing-hampton-village-store-in-st-louis-holding-liquidation-sale/article_82e78e79-8ffe-52b6-abb0-65f081576ae0.html

Macklind Business District https://macklindbdstl.com/ Accessed February 12, 2022.

Old Maps on Line https://www.oldmapsonline.org/map/harvard/11261201 Accessed Feb. 7, 2021, February 15 2021 and other dates.

South Side Journal, March 6, 2002,April 21, 2002, September 12, 2007.

St. Louis Post-Dispatch, October 6, 1923, December 2, 1923, September 1, 1932, January 30, 1939 November 30, 1962, March 11, 1964, December 27, 1964, June 27, 1965, October 31, 1967, and June 29, 1969, September 11, 1976, November 24, 2002.

Holt, Dr. Glen and Pearson, Tom,St. Louis Streets Index, St. Louis Public Library, http://rbsc.slpl.org/STL_STREETS_(A-Z).pdf, accessed Feb. 22, 2021.

Ted Drewes website, http://teddrewes.com/, accessed Feb, 17, 2021 and other times.

Southampton Neighborhood Association/History https://www.southamptonstl.org/Neighborhood-History Accessed February 10, 2022.

Stevens, Josh, email to author, August 20, 2021.

Stltoday, June 28, 2013.

I Follow a Real Estate Genius

Elz, Ron, written document on St. Louis Hills, and interview, July 20, 2021.

Francis Park, Overview and amenities for Francis Park, https://www.stlouis-mo.gov/government/departments/parks/parks/browse-parks/view-park.cfm?parkID=3&parkName=Francis%20Park, Accessed July 30, 2021.

News of St. Louis Hills, undated issue in 1952.

St. Gabriel the Archangel Catholic Church website, https://www.stgabrielstl.org, Accessed July 7, 2021.

Ohlendorf Park https://stlouiscountymo.gov/st-louis-county-departments/parks/about/park-history-documents/ohlendorf-history/, Accessed January 24, 2022.

Palank, Rick, interview, July 20, 2021.

Paul Ritter, interview.

St. Louis Post-Dispatch, Nov. 21, 1920, May 21, 1922. May 2, 1928, July 20, 1930. Dec. 21, 1930 July 9, 1950, Nov. 2, 1981, Nov. 18, 1985, April 11, 1949, Nov. 17, 1935, Dec. 27, 1916.

St. Raphael Parish website, St. Raphael the Archangel Parish Https://www.st raphael archangel.org/, Accessed July 27, 2021.

Ritter, Paul interview, July 20, 2021.

Saracino, Chris, interview.

Sauce Magazine Website, Rockwell Beer Garden brings new pizza-centric program to Francis Park, July 29, 2021, https://www.saucemagazine.com/a/59435/rockwell-beer-garden-brings-new-pizza-centric-program-to-fra?fbclid=IwAR1cJfxXftnCfHWvLKW9LZsD1dXkvtXjnHE5pOn4qeIkucXmtA2Yim1Jwt8 Accessed July 30, 2021.

St. Louis Hills Neighborhood Association website, https://stlhills.com/, Accessed July 27, 2021.

Barnes, Harper, Standing on a Volcano: The Life and Times of David Rowland Francis (St. Louis: Missouri Historical Society Press 2001) https://www.amazon.com/Standing-Volcano-Times-

Rowland-Francis/dp/1883982170, Accessed July 12, 2021.

St. Louis Cultural Resources Office Neighborhood Histories, Neighborhood Histories by Norbury L. Wayman published in 1978, https://www.stlouis-mo.gov/government/departments/planning/cultural-resources/neighborhood-histories.cfm, Accessed July 12, 2021, and various other times.

Vordtriede, Nancy, January 19, 2022 - January 26, 2022, emails to the author. July 20, 2021.

Willmore Park, Overview and Amenities for Willmore Park, https://www.stlouis-mo.gov/government/departments/parks/parks/browse-parks/vie

w-park.cfm?parkID=93&parkName=Willmore%20Park, Accessed July 30, 2021.

Rows of Graves and a Windmill

Arkadin Cinema website, https://arkadincinema.com/, Accessed August 28, 2021.

Concordia Turners website, http://www.concordiaturners.org/, Accessed August 28, 2021.

Das Bevo Facebook page, Accessed August 28, 2021.

Das Bevo website, http://dasbevo.com/, Accessed August 28, 2021.

The Heavy Anchor Bar & Venue, https://www.theheavyanchor.com/, Accessed August 28, 2021.

The History of Gateway Gardens Cemetery https://www.stlouis-mo.gov/government/departments/sldc/real-estate/gatewood-gardens-cemetery/gatewood-gardens-history.cfm.

Kratz, Gary, interview, August 19, 2021.

Kukic, Sadik, interview, September 14, 2021.

"Larry," Interview.

MetroSTL.com, July 23, 2021, Miniature Museum makes it big by thinking small. https://metrostl.com/2021/07/24/miniature-museum-makes-it-big-by-thinking-small/

Oak Hill Elementary School. https://www.slps.org/Page/40778, Accessed November 24, 2021.

Ottinger, David, interview, August 26, 2021.

Plaque in front of South St. Louis Memorial Post 37, 4617 Dahlia Ave., next to cannon display.

Richie, Roger, interview, August 19, 2021.

South Side Cyclery, The Chappuis-Blackwood Family, https://www.southsidecyclery.com/articles/our-history-pg196.htm, Accessed, September 18, 2021.

St. Louis Streets Index, http://rbsc.slpl.org/STL_STREETS_(A-Z).pdf, Accessed Aug. 20-22, 2021.

St. Louis Magazine, Das Bevo, the former Bevo Mill, opens in South City, https://www.stlmag.com/dining/das-bevo-the-former-bevo-mill-opens-in%20south-city/

St. Louis Post-Dispatch Nov. 22, 1916.

Stltoday, September 30, 2013.

Timbrook, Jodie, interview, August 26, 2021.

Search City of St. Louis Ordinances, https://www.stlouis-mo.gov/government/city-laws/ordinances/search.cfm?q

Merkel, Jim, Beer, Brats, and Baseball, 1st edition (St. Louis, Reedy Press, 2012).

Three Sides of Tower Grove South

Burbridge, Josh, and Weil, Andrew, From Prairie to Destination: The Story of South Grand, https://southgrand.org/

Green, Chris, interview.

Johnson, Walter, The Broken Heart of America: St. Louis and the Violent History of the United States, (Basic Books, Illustrated edition 2020)

Mackney, Jolie, interview, September 12, 2021.

MoFo Residences, https://www.moforesidences.com/, Accessed September 12, 2021.

New Apartments signify resurgence of Morgan Ford Business District, https://metrostl.com/2019/05/17/new-apartments-signify-resurgence-of-morgan-ford-business-district/, Accessed September 12, 2021.

Prapaisilp, Suchin, interview.

Road Crew Coffee and Cycles, https://www.roadcrew.cc/, Accessed September 12, 2021.

Rosicrucian Order, https://www.rosicrucian.org/

South Grand, http://southgrand.org, Accessed September 13, 2021, January 1, 2022.

Thinking of Marti Frumhoff While Accepting My Own Mortality, https://www.urbanreviewstl.com/2021/05/thinking-of-marti-frumhoff-while-accepting-my-own-mortality/, Accessed September 10, 2021.

Witt, Rachel.

An Old Shopping District Stays Alive

Beer, Brats, and Baseball: St. Louis Germans,, 1st Edition (St. Louis, Reedy Press, 2012.

Big Experiment in Adaptive Reuse.

https://www.huffpost.com/entry/jason-deems-on-st-louis-a_b_4738016, accessed March 21, 2021.

Brannon, Pat, interview.

Britannica, Osceola, Seminole Leader, Accessed Oct. 4, 2021.

Chatillon-DeMenil Mansion, https://www.demenil.org/. Accessed March 21, 2021.

Chatillon-DeMenil House, https://npgallery.nps.gov/AssetDetail/53d7d77c-8749-4c25-8f8f-a8ddcc1ed6bc, Accessed March 21, 2021.

The Cheshire Grin Cat Cafe, https://thecheshiregrincatcafe.com/, accessed March 17, 2021.

Christman, Bill, interview.

Deem, Jason, interview, March 21, 2021.

Dead Wax Records STL Facebook Page, accessed March 17, 2021.

Elder, Cherri, interview, March 30, 2021.

Explore St. Louis - Cherokee Street https://explorestlouis.com/partner/cherokee-street/

Hammonds Books, https://hammondsbooks.net/, accessed March 17, 2021.

Heagney, Adele, Reference Librarian, Central Library, St. Louis Public Library, email to author, March 7, 2021.

The Lemp Mansion Restaurant and Inn, https://www.lempmansion.com/, Accessed March 22, 2021.

The Mud House, www.themudhousestl.com, accessed March 17, 2021.

NATIONAL REGISTER OF HISTORIC PLACES INVENTORY .... NOMINATION FORM, Chatillon-DeMenil House, https://dnr.mo.gov/shpo/nps-nr/78001673.pdf, Accessed March 21, 2021.

Seeaghost.com, website of St. Louis Paranormal Research Society, accessed March 17, 2021.

Stltoday.com June 1, 2007, March 22, 2014.

STL Rocks, https://www.stlrocks.me/, accessed March 17, 2021.

Thenhaus, Emily, interview, March 21, 2021.

Simon, Ray, interview, March 21, 2021.

Vines. Randy, interview, March 12, 2021.

Vines, Randy, emails to author, October 4, 2021, September 28, 2021, September 27, 2021.

1956 St. Louis City Directory.

Celebration, Boxing, and Farmers at a Market

American Battlefield Trust: Nathaniel Lyon, https://www.battlefields.org/learn/biographies/nathaniel-lyon, Accessed June 15, 2022.

Button, Mike, interview, March 3, 2021.

Citywide Neighborhoods Map-2, https://www.stlouis-mo.gov/government/departments/planning/documents/upload/CitywideNeighborhoodMap-2.pdf, Accessed June 15, 2021.

Civil War Era: The Contested Memories of General Nathaniel Lyon in St. Louis. By Nick Sacco May 28, 2019, https://www.journalofthecivilwarera.org/2019/05/the-contested-memories-of-general-nathaniel-lyon-in-st-louis/, Accessed June 15, 2022.

Does St. Louis have the second-largest Mardi Gras in the US?

https://www.ksdk.com/article/news/verify/verify-second-largest-mardi-gras-us-st-louis/63-0cd37a81-af8d-47c9-9fca-f0223c20b42f, Accessed: March 2, 2022.

General Nathaniel Lyon Monument, https://www.stlouis-mo.gov/government/departments/parks/parks/browse-parks/amenity.cfm Accessed June 10, 2021.

Gibbs, Jay, interview.

Guenther, Dan, interview, March, 3, 2021.

Holloran, Jim, interview, April 29, 2022.

Lyon Park Amenities, https://www.stlouis-mo.gov/parks/parks/browse-parks/view-park.cfm?parkID=8&parkName=Lyon%20Park&amenitySubTypeID=27, Accessed June 10, 2021.

National Register of Historic Places Inventory - Nomination Form, Soulard Neighborhood Historic District. https://dnr.mo.gov/shpo/nps-nr/72001559.pdf, Accessed June 13, 2021.

Soulard Mardi Gras https://www.ksdk.com/article/news/local/soulard-mardi-gras-parade-2022/63-adee9202-ff9f-4684-b2b7-58b0b85bcc53, Accessed March 6, 2022.

Soulard Market STL. Soulard Market STL.http://soulardmarketstl.com, Accessed, June 15, 2022.

Soulard http://soulardmarketstl.com / Overview, City of St. Louis website, https://www.stlouis-mo.gov/live-work/community/neighborhoods/soulard/soulard-overview.cfm, Accessed June 13, 2021.

South Broadway Athletic Club website, https://www.sbacstl.org/, Accessed June 15, 2021.

Wilkins, Kevin, interview, March 7, 2021.

How Soulard became the Mardi Gras party capital of St. Louis, https://www.ksdk.com/article/syndication/podcasts/soulard-mardi-gras-st-louis-history/63-72f00cc2-add6-4809-b185-e9a659da5d24, Accessed March 6, 2022.

St. Louis Magazine, tour of Busch Plant.

Merkel, Jim, Unique Homes of St. Louis. Unpublished Manuscript.

Primm, James Neal, Lion of the Valley: St. Louis, Missouri, 1764-1980 (Missouri History Museum Press; Third edition, December 1, 1998).

Busch ADS, https://www.youtube.com/watch?v=vZbK_ZrAgzI

https://www.youtube.com/watch?v=vl1EcSnXPQA

https://www.youtube.com/watch?v=Kln168tvCFg

Lafayette Square: Life in a Museum

Brainerd, Jim, interview.

Bryan, John Albury, Lafayette Square: St. Louis Reedy Press, 2007.

Clementine's Creamery Naughty and Nice, https://www.clementinescreamery.com/flavors/, Accessed April 14, 2021.

Conley, Timothy G., Lafayette Square: An Urban Renaissance St. Louis, Lafayette Square Press, January 1, 1974.

Fields Foods, http://www.fieldsfoods.com/, Accessed June 10, 2021.

The Georgian, http://gilded-age.com/georgian.html, Accessed June 10, 2021.

Kamphoefner, Ruth, Lafayette Comes Back (St. Louis, self-published, 2000).

Lafayette Park Conservancy, http://lafayettepark.org/, Accessed April 4, 2021.

Lafayette Park Playgrounds, https://lafayettepark.org/playground/, Accessed April 9, 2021.

Lafayette Square, https://www.lafayettesquare.org, Accessed May 10, 2022.

Lafayette Square, https://www.stlouis-mo.gov/archive/neighborhood-histories-norbury-wayman/lafayette/park16.htm, Accessed April 9, 2021.

Lafayette Square Historic District, https://www.stlouis-mo.gov/government/departments/planning/cultural-resources/Lafayette-Square-Historic-District.cfm, Accessed September 28, 2022.

Lafayette Park George Washington Statue, https://www.stlouis-mo.gov/parks/parks/browse-parks/amenity.cfm?id=462, April 8, 2021.

Lafayette Park Vintage Base Ball Field, Facebook page, accessed April 6, 2021.

Merkel, Jim, Unique Homes of St. Louis. Unpublished Manuscript.

St. Louis Cultural Resources Office, Lafayette Square Historic District, https://www.stlouis-mo.gov/government/departments/planning/cultural-resources/Lafayette-Square-Historic-District.cfm, Accessed April 19, 2021.

Hahn, Andrew, interview with author, April 16, 2021.

McGuffey House and Museum, https://www.miamioh.edu/cca/mcguffey-museum/miami-oxford-history/george-washington-statue/#:~:text=The%20original%20marble%20statue%20was%20completed%20in%201792,molds%20made%20from%20a%20mask%20of%20Washington-%E2%80%99s%20face., Accessed, April 8, 2021.

Merkel, Jim, The Colorful Characters of St. Louis. St. Louis, Reedy Press, 2016.

Murphy, Tom, interview.

Negri, Matt, interview.

NEXT STL Big Plans for Chouteau in Lafayette Square https://nextstl.com/2018/03/big-plans-for-chouteau-in-lafayette-square/, accessed April 5, 2021.

NextSTL HARLAND BARTHOLOMEW: DESTROYER OF THE URBAN FABRIC OF ST. LOUIS, April 10, 2021, NextSTL: Big Plans for Chouteau in Lafayette Square. https://nextstl.com/2018/03/big-plans-for-chouteau-in-lafayette-square/, Accessed April 19, 2021, and other days.

https://nextstl.com/2021/04/harland-bartholomew-destroyer-of-the-urban-fabric-of-st-louis/ , Accessed June 13, 2021.

Ozlah, Ugur, interview.

Polite Society website, https://www.politesocietystl.com/#landing Accessed April 14, 2021.

Revolutionary War Cannons, https://www.stlouis-mo.gov/parks/parks/browse-parks/amenity.cfm?id=87, Accessed April 7, 2021.

David Ramsey Map Collections, Rand McNally and Company, Rand, McNally & Co.'s St. Louis. (with) Map of St. Louis and Vicinity.

1903, https://www.oldmapsonline.org/map/rumsey/2844.058 Accessed March 20, 2022.

St. Louis Streets Index, http://rbsc.slpl.org/STL_STREETS_(A-Z).pdf

St. Louis Post-Dispatch, January 4, 1959, June 7, 1960.

Sessions, Suzanne, interview.

SqWires Restaurant website, https://sqwires.com/dinner-menu/, Accessed April 14, 2021.

Umsted, Jared, interview.

Westward on Chouteau and Manchester

Bradley, Mike, interview.

Cinema Treasures Manchester Theatre, St. Louis https://beekman.herokuapp.com/theaters/6965 .

Danforth William H. Tribute, Milestones, https://rememberingbilldanforth.wustl.edu/legacy/milestones/ Accessed April 27, 2022.

The Grove, https://www.thegrovestl.com/

HandleBar 4127 Manchester Avenue, https://www.toasttab.com/handlebar-4127-manchester-ave/v3https://www.toasttab.com/handlebar-4127-manchester-ave/v, Accessed March 2022.

Phillips, Brian, interview, March 16, 2022.

Park Central Development, https://parkcentraldevelopment.org/ Accessed March 16, 2022.

A hobby takes flight: How one man built a collection of historic military planes in St. Louis, https://www.stltoday.com/news/local/metro/a-hobby-takes-flight-how-one-man-built-a-collection-of-historic-military-planes-in/article_9806c3a0-9cc1-59c8-b913-f7c1457c72a0.html Accessed March 16, 2022.

Efficient Plant Process Safety: Train On Safe Gas-Cylinder Handling, EP Editorial Staff, October 21, 2009, https://www.efficientplantmag.com/2009/10/process-safety-train-on-safe-gas-cylinder-handling/ Accessed March 16, 2022.

$160M redevelopment of former Praxair site to start construction, https://www.bizjournals.com/stlouis/news/2019/04/18/160m-redevelopment-of-former-praxair-site-to.html, Accessed March 31, 2022.

Man charged with conspiracy to use Interstate Commerce Facilities in the Commission of Murder-for-Hire, Resulting in Death, https://www.justice.gov/usao-edmo/pr/man-charged-conspiracy-use-interstate-commerce-facilities-commission-murder-hire, Accessed March, 2022.

One of area's largest caterers adding event space in The Grove St. Louis Business Journal, November 11, 2019.

Park Central Development website, https://parkcentraldevelopment.org/, Accessed March, 2022.

Safety Bulletin, US Chemical Safety and Hazard Investigation Board, Fire at Praxair St. Louis: Dangers of Propylene Cylinders in High Temperatures, June 2006. file:///C:/Users/James%20Merkel/Desktop/Praxair_Report%20(1).pdf.

Syracuse, Brandon, nextstl.com, January 17, 2021.

Slay, Guy, interview.

Stltoday, June 3, 2022, September 26, 2022, October. 20, 2022.

On the Road of Tamm and the Avenue of Oaks

The Pat Connolly Tavern, https://www.patconnollytavern.com/ Accessed September 28, 2002.

Seamus McDaniel's, https://seamusmcdaniels.com/, Accessed September 28, 2022.

Turtle Playground, http://www.forestparkstatues.org/turtle-playground, accessed April 9, 2021.

St. Louis Catholic School to Close. https://metrostl.com/2019/02/16/st-james-catholic-school-to-close/, Accessed April 20, 2022.

Bob Corbett's Dogtown Homepage http://faculty.webster.edu/corbetre/dogtown/dogtown.html Accessed March 19, 2022.

Corbett, Bob, interview, March 19, 2022.

David Ramsey Map Collections, Rand McNally and Company, Rand, McNally & Co.'s St. Louis. (with) Map of St. Louis and Vicinity.

Corbett, John, interview.

1903, https://www.oldmapsonline.org/map/rumsey/2844.058, Accessed March 20, 2022.

Forest Park Statues and Monuments: Turtle Playground, http://www.forestparkstatues.org/turtle-playground, Accessed March 2022.

History of St. Louis Neighborhoods By Norbury L. Wayman, Oakland https://www.stlouis-mo.gov/archive/neighborhood-histories-norbury-wayman/oakland/streets21.htm

Jovanovich, Joe, interview.

Lost Tables: Stan Musial & Biggie's, https://www.losttables.com/musial/musial.htm, Accessed March 2022.

Merkel, Jim Hoosiers and Scrubby Dutch: St. Louis's South Side, St. Louis: Reedy Press: 2010, St. Louis

MetroSTL.com 36th Annual Hibernian Parade coming to Dogtown.

March 14, 2019, Last Updated: March 16, 2019.

https://metrostl.com/2019/03/14/36th-annual-hibernian-parade-coming-to-dogtown/, Accessed October 26, 2021.

The Pat Connolly Tavern, https://www.patconnollytavern.com/, Accessed March 2022.

Police Circus, Three Stooges, Accessed March 2022.

Red Feather Legacy, http://www.communitychest.org.za/2017-06-29-14-37-22/legacy-partners.html, Accessed March 14, 2022.

Remembering Forest Park Highlands Amusement Park https://fox2now.com/news/fox-files/remembering-forest-park-highlands-amusement-park/Accessed March 22, 2022.

St. Louis Arena Implosion | Living St. Louis.

Stltoday, May 15, 2020.

https://www.youtube.com/watch?v=WPr9DapNd3c, Accessed March 22, 2022.

St. Louis Arena Demolition.

https://www.youtube.com/watch?v=yV_2aOQRkeo, Accessed March 22, 2022.

St. Louis Magazine: St. Louis Sage: How Did Dogtown Get Its Name? https://www.stlmag.com/news/st-louis-sage-how-did-dogtown-get-its-name/, Accessed Oct. 25, 2021.

The Stan Musial Tour of St. Louis https://www.riverfronttimes.com/stlouis/the-stan-musial-tour-of-st-louis/Content?oid=2585473 Accessed March 22, 2022.

Stan Musial and Biggie's St. Louis https://dfarq.homeip.net/stan-musial-and-biggies-st-louis/ Accessed March 22, 2022.

St. Louis Patina, Old Deaconess Hospital, Posted on April 24, 2012 by Chris Naffziger, Accessed October 24, 2021.

St. Louis Streets Index (March 1994) http://rbsc.slpl.org/STL_STREETS_(A-Z).pdf, Accessed March 2022.

Stlracing.com. Accessed May 1, 2022.

Stltoday.com, May 27, 2008, February 19, 2009, December 5, 2012, October 20, 2016, January 2, 2018, May 15, 2020, September 2, 2021, March 12, 2022.

Winter tornado tears through St. Louis https://www.ksdk.com/article/entertainment/television/ksdk-75-years/deadly-1959-winter-tornado-st-louis-tore-arena-roof/63-9324834f-ca14-4652-b089-469cb3180544, Accessed March 2022.

All Things Italian

Aiazzi, Joan, interviews by author and emails, July, 2022.

Alexander, LynnMarie, interviews.

Apostles of the Sacred Heart of Jesus, https://www.ascjus.org/, Accessed January 28, 2021.

America's Last Little Italy: The Hill. https://www.amazon.com/Americas-Last-Little-Italy-Hill/dp/B08PFSRF5P Accessed November 3, 2021.

Carnivore STL https://www.carnivore-stl.com/ Accessed May 18, 2022.

Bommarito, Monsignor Vincent, interview.

DeGregorio, Joseph, interviews and emails at various times.

DiGregorio, Frank, interview.

Lorenzo's Trattoria http://lorenzostrattoria.com/, Accessed May 2022.

Explore St. Louis: The Hill https://explorestlouis.com/things-to-do/neighborhoods/the-hill/, Accessed, January 30, 2022.

Fazzio's Since 1902, https://www.faziosbakery.com/bakery-items-specialty-productsAccessed November 1, 2021.

Gia Ristorante Italiano, http://www.giaristorante.com/, January 27, 2022.

The Hill https://www.hillstl.org/ Accessed May 2022.

The Hill Apartments, https://www.hollandcs.com/portfolio/the-hill-apartments

The Hill Apartments, https://explorestlouis.com/things-to-do/neighborhoods/the-hill/, Accessed January 30, 2022.

Hoover, Dea, interviews.

The Italian Immigrants, By Rudolph Torrini, https://explorestlouis.com/things-to-do/neighborhoods/the-hill/, Accessed January 30, 2022.

Merkel, Jim, Hoosiers and Scrubby Dutch: St. Louis's South Side, 1st Edition, (St. Louis, Reedy Press, 2010).

Milo's Bocce Garden, https://www.milosboccegarden.com/history/the-wall/, Accessed November 27, 2022.

Missouri Baking Company Menu.

https://restaurantguru.com/Missouri-Baking-Co-St-Louis/menu Accessed November 1, 2021.

New Piazza Imo to open in iconic Hill neighborhood on Sunday.

https://fox2now.com/news/new-piazza-imo-to-open-in-iconic-hill-neighborhood-on-sunday/ Accessed November 1, 2021.

Piazza Imo https://www.piazzaimo.com/, Accessed May 14, 2022 and July 26, 2022.

Piazza Imo dedication in The Hill stirs joy, thanksgiving.

https://metrostl.com/2019/08/19/piazza-imo-dedication-in-the-hill-stirs-joy-thanksgiving/, Accessed January 27, 2022.

O'Connell's Pub, https://www.oconnells-pub.com/, Accessed November 1, 2021.

Ribaudo, Toni, interview.

Rigazzi's, https://www.rigazzis.com/

Sacred Heart Villa, History, https://www.sacredheartvilla.org/About/History, Accessed June 26, 2022 and November 1, 2021.

Schmitt, Lois, emails to author, various times in July 2022.

Shaw's Coffee, https://shawscoffee.com/ Accessed November 2, 2021.

2nd Shift Brewing, http://www.2ndshiftbrewing.com/about/ Accessed November 1, 2021.

Shop Local on the Hill https://www.hillstl.org/shop-local-on-the-hill/, Accessed November 3, 2021.

Stltoday, September 23, 2015. March 14, 2017.

Tours offer inside look at city's Hill neighborhood.

https://metrostl.com/2019/09/10/tours-offer-inside-look-at-citys-hill-neighborhood/, Accessed January 30, 2022.

What is Bocce Ball? https://www.thespruce.com/what-is-bocce-ball-2736598, Accessed January 27, 2022.

Henry Shaw's Masterpiece

Missouri Botanical Garden: Our History https://www.missouribotanicalgarden.org/about/additional-information/our-history.aspx, Accessed February 27, 2022.

In honor of Juneteenth, Missouri Botanical Garden lists names of slaves owned by Garden founder Henry Shaw, June `19, 2020. https://www.stltoday.com/news/local/metro/in-honor-of-juneteenth-missouri-botanical-garden-lists-names-of-slaves-owned-by-garden-founder/article_98d6fc4f-648e-53c3-9683-8d93a28fe7bf.html Accessed April 26, 2022.

Missouri Botanical Garden: Who Was Henry Shaw? https://www.missouribotanicalgarden.org/media/fact-pages/who-was-henry-shaw.aspx Accessed February 27, 2022.

https://www.missouribotanicalgarden.org/media/fact-pages/who-was-henry-shaw.aspx Accessed February 27, 2022.

Ices Plain & Fancy: https://icesplainandfancy.com/ Accessed February 27, 2022.

Gerstner, Jenny, interview, February 2022.

Sonntag, Michael, interview, February 25, 2022.

History of St. Louis Neighborhoods, Shaw, by Norbury Wayman, https://www.stlouis-mo.gov/archive/neighborhood-histories-norbury-wayman/shaw/land28.htm, Accessed February 22, 2022.

Missouri Botanical Garden, https://www.missouribotanicalgarden.org/

https://www.missouribotanicalgarden.org/

Missouri Botanical Garden: Who was Henry Shaw? https://www.missouribotanicalgarden.org/media/fact-pages/who-was-henry-shaw.aspx, Accessed November 6, 2021.

Doyle, Amanda, emails to author, February 2022.

Bill Reininger, interview with author, February 24, 2022.

Tower Grove Park website, https://www.towergroveparkmap.org/, Access June 9, 2022.

Twain, Mark, Life on the Mississippi, www.gutenberg.org, Release Date: August 20, 2006 [EBook #245]
Last Updated: February 24, 2018.

Tower Grove Farmers Market web site, https://tgfarmersmarket.com/, Accessed June 30, 2022

Tower Grove Park website, https://www.towergrovepark.org/ Accessed June 30, 2022.

Tower Grove Park Overview and Amenities for Tower Grove Park. https://www.
stlouis-mo.gov/government/departments/parks/parks/browse-parks/view-park.
cfm?parkID=115&parkName=Tower+Grove+Park Accessed Nov. 8, 2021.

GPS technology zooms in on Tower Grove Park trees.

Jim Merkel, June 21, 2019, https://metrostl.com/2019/06/21/gps-technology-zooms-in-on-tower-
grove-park-trees/ Accessed Nov. 8, 2021.

Missouri Botanical Garden, https://www.missouribotanicalgarden.org/, Accessed Nov. 8, 2021.

Tower Grove Park https://www.towergrovepark.org/, Accessed Nov. 8, 2021.

Columbus statue taken down in Tower Grove Park in St. Louis Jun 17, 2020.

Stltoday, https://www.stltoday.com/news/local/crime-and-courts/columbus-statue-taken-down-in-
tower-grove-park-in-st-louis/article_94764b8c-8b49-536e-bc45-fb7d856b7ce9.html, Accessed, Nov.
11, 2021.

Columbus Statue, Tower Grove Park, https://www.stltoday.com/news/local/crime-and-courts/
columbus-statue-taken-down-in-tower-grove-park-in-st-louis/article_94764b8c-8b49-536e-bc45-
fb7d856b7ce9.html, Accessed Nov. 11, 2021.

 St. Louis Public Radio: Take 5: Another look at Henry Shaw as his 213th birthday approaches.

https://www.stlmag.com/Compton-Heights/, Accessed January 5, 2022.

History of St. Louis Neighborhoods by Norbury L. Wayman, https://www.stlouis-mo.gov/archive/
neighborhood-histories-norbury-wayman/compton/index10.htm, Accessed January 5, 2022.

History of Shaw: https://shawstlouis.org/all-about-shaw/history/, Accessed January 5, 2022.

Mansions and a Town of Strings

ST. LOUIS STREETS INDEX (1994) by Dr. Glen Holt and Tom Pearson St. Louis Public Library
http://rbsc.slpl.org/STL_STREETS_(A-Z).pdf, Accessed January 5, 2022.

Merkel, Jim: Hoosiers and Scrubby Dutch. 2nd Edition St. Louis, Reedy Press, 2014.

The Fleur-de-Lys Mansion, https://www.thefleurdelys.com/, Accessed November 12, 2021.

Cultural Resources Office.

Naked Truth Statue - City Landmark #27.

https://www.stlouis-mo.gov/government/departments/planning/cultural-resources/city-landmarks/
Naked-Truth-Statue-Place.cfm, Accessed November 12, 2021.

(St. Louis) Cultural Resources Office.

Compton Heights Neighborhood Betterment Association, http://comptonheights.org/ Accessed
February 27, 2022.

Compton Hill Water Tower https://mostateparks.com/sites/mostateparks/files/Compton%20Hill%20
Water%20Tower.pdf Accessed February 27, 2022.

Compton Hill Water Tower - City Landmark #13.

https://docs.google.com/document/d/1OeiBELNZ3uv2XMlTWsEDaMcv-9p5SaCztUIgEG38qks/
edit#, Accessed November 12, 2021.

Magic Chef Mansion, https://docs.google.com/document/d/1OeiBELNZ3uv2XMlTWsEDaMcv-
9p5SaCztUIgEG38qks/edit#, Accessed November 12, 2021.

ST. LOUIS STREETS INDEX St. Louis Public Library http://rbsc.slpl.org/STL_STREETS_(A-Z).pdf,
Accessed January 5, 2022.

Abandoned Historic Virginia Theater https://www.thetelegraph.com/projects/2022/visuals/abandoned-
virginia-theater-tour/, Accessed June 27, 2022.

Overview and amenities for Gravois Park, https://www.stlouis-mo.gov/parks/parks/browse-parks/
view-park.cfm?parkID=46&parkName=Gravois%20Park, Accessed November 16, 2021.

St. Anthony of Padua Catholic Church http://www.stanthonyofpaduastl.com/ Accessed November 16,
2021.

Overview and amenities for Marquette Park.

https://www.stlouis-mo.gov/parks/parks/browse-parks/view-park.cfm?parkID=59, Accessed November 16, 2021.

Feasting Fox in Dutchtown, Oct 21, 2020.

https://www.stltoday.com/feasting-fox-in-dutchtown/article_3e0063aa-3d3a-5488-81ae-0a290d2fd1e2.html, Accessed November 16, 2021.

William McKinley.

https://www.history.com/topics/us-presidents/william-mckinley, Accessed: November 16, 2021.

Merkel, Jim Unpublished manuscript Unique Homes of St. Louis.

St. Louis Post-Dispatch July 9, 1995, February 10, 1957, August 30, 1966, November 3, 1972, September 20, 1989, November 17, 1990.

Anthony Duncan Architect LLC, https://www.duncanarchitecture.com/, Accessed November 18, 2021.

Roosevelt High School, Home of the Rough Riders, https://www.slps.org/domain/5317, Accessed November 18, 2021.

Cinema Treasures, Virginia Theatre, 5117 Virginia Avenue, St. Louis, MO 63111, http://cinematreasures.org/theaters/4955, Accessed Nov. 18, 2021.

Carondelet Neighborhood Map.

Duncan, Anthony, interview, January 19, 2022.

https://www.stlouis-mo.gov/government/departments/planning/documents/Carondelet-nghbrhd-map.cfm, Accessed November 19, 2021.

We Buy Ugly Houses, https://www.webuyuglyhouses.com/, Accessed November 19, 2021.

Overview and amenities for Gravois Park, https://www.stlouis-mo.gov/parks/parks/browse-parks/view-park.cfm?parkID=46&parkName=Gravois%20Park, Accessed November 16, 2021.

South Side Journal, June 24, 1998.

St. Louis Streets Index, St. Louis Public Library, http://rbsc.slpl.org/STL_STREETS_(A-Z).pdf, accessed January 19, 2021.

My Jaunt Through the Town of Empty Pockets

Bellerive Park: Overview and Amenities for Bellerive Park, https://www.stlouis-mo.gov/government/departments/parks/parks/browse-parks/view-park.cfm?parkID=16&parkName=Bellerive%20Park, Accessed April 28, 2021.

Built St. Louis: The South Side: Carondelet https://www.builtstlouis.net/southside/carondelet13.html, Accessed May 17, 2021.

Carondelet Historical Marker, https://www.hmdb.org/m.asp?m=139705

CarondeletLiving.com, Murals on Broadway, https://www.carondeletliving.com/murals, Accessed May 17, 2021.

For Carondelet's Seventh Mural on Broadway, Carondelet was a Clear Pick, Riverfront Times, April 4, 2016. https://www.riverfronttimes.com/artsblog/2016/04/04/for-carondelets-seventh-mural-on-broadway-clark-terry-was-a-clear-pick, Accessed May 18, 2021.

Deariing, Jayme, interviews.

Dedication to James B. Eads, https://www.hmdb.org/m.asp?m=139710, Accessed May 19, 2021.

Jefferson Barracks Heritage Foundation, History, http://jbhf.org/jeffersonbarracks/history.html, Accessed May 19, 2021.

Merkel, Jim, Hoosiers and Scrubby Dutch: 2nd Edition, 2014.

Primm, James Neal, Lion of the Valley: St. Louis, Missouri. 1981

Hessel, Fred, interview, May 20, 2020.

Moore, David, interviews.

Sisters of St. Joseph of Carondelet, Carondelet Community Comes Together for Mural Painting, https://www.csjsl.org/news/carondelet-community-comes-together-for-mural-paiting, Accessed, May 24, 2021.

Historic Carondelet Living: Murals on Broadway. https://www.carondeletliving.com/murals, Accessed May 24, 2021.

National Register of Historic Places Inventory - Nomination Form. Convent of the Sisters of St. Joseph of_Carondelet. https://dnr.mo.gov/shpo/nps-nr/80004505.pdf Accessed May 25, 2021.

Sinkhole website, http://sinkholerecords.com/, Accessed May 26, 2021.

Stacked Burger Bar website, https://www.stackedstl.com/, Accessed May 26, 2021.

Sisters of St. Joseph of Carondelet St. Louis Province, website, https://www.csjsl.org/, Accessed May 26, 2021.

Stltoday, January 11, 2011.

Graffiti, a Lake, and Gravestones in a Park

Alexander Lyle House, https://www.stlhistoryandarchitecture.com/carondelet/x186p66tt299ztkzfb03iecwabyrr7, Accessed December 9, 2021.

Allen, Michael R. The Harnessed Channel: How the River Des Peres Became a Sewer, http://preservationresearch.com/infrastructure/the-harnessed-channel-how-the-river-des-peres-became-a-sewer/ Accessed various times, including May 8, 2022.

Carondelet Park: Overview and Amenities for Carondelet Park https://www.stlouis-mo.gov/government/departments/parks/parks/browse-parks/view-park.cfm?parkID=5, Accessed December 2021.

Duncan, Anthony, interview, January 19, 2022.

EAA AirVenture Oshkosh 2012: Blue Angels Leader F/A-18C Hornet.

https://aeroexperience.blogspot.com/2012/12/eaa-airventure-oshkosh-2012-blue-angels.html, Accessed January 1, 2022.

Fitzer, Jeffrey, interview, January 11, 2022.

Is Graffiti Art or Vandalism? March 3, 2018. https://graffitiknowhow.com/is-graffiti-art-or-vandalism/ Accessed December 6, 2021.

Seitz, Geoffrey, interview, January 11 2022.

Accessed December 15, 2021.

Greenway Plans and Projects https://greatriversgreenway.org/plans-and-projects/, Accessed November 27, 2021.

Great Rivers Greenway website https://greatriversgreenway.org, Accessed Dec. 6, 2021 and other dates.

Old St. Marcus Cemetery, https://www.findagrave.com/cemetery/30670/old-saint-marcus-cemetery, Accessed December 7, 2021.

Stltoday, February 2, 2010, November 7, 2021.

St. Marcus Commemorative Park https://www.stlouis-mo.gov/parks/parks/browse-parks/view-park.cfm?parkID=80, Accessed December 7, 2021.

St. Louis Urban Fishing Program Lakes, https://mdc.mo.gov/fishing/fishing-prospects/areas/st-louis-urban-fishing-program-lakes, Accessed December 3, 2021.

Photo Flood 9: Carondelet Park http://www.photofloodstl.org/photo-flood-9-carondelet-park/, Accessed December 3, 2021.

River des Peres Greenway Master Plan https://greatriversgreenway.org/river-des-peres-greenway-master-plan/ Accessed November 27, 2021.

What Is Street Art? Its History, Definition, Purpose, and Importance, https://davidcharlesfox.com/what-is-street-art-history-definition-purpose-importance/, Accessed Dec. 6, 2021.

Little Guys Hold the Line on Hampton

Area 51 http://www.smoketalk.net/smokeshops/mo/saint-louis/area-51, Accessed January 11, 2022.

Buder Branch, St. Louis Public Library, http://www.stlouiscitytalk.com/posts/2016/01/buder-branch-of-st-louis-public-library, Accessed December 13, 2021.

Find a Grave Andrew "Cap" Tilles, https://www.findagrave.com/memorial/149398407/andrew-tilles, Accessed December 14, 2021.

Haffner, Jean, interview.

Hampton Gardens apartments will pay more to occupy site. February 24, 2020, https://metrostl.com/2020/02/24/hampton-gardens-apartments-will-pay-more-to-occupy-site/, Accessed December 16, 2021.

Lost Tables Velvet Freeze, https://www.losttables.com/vfreeze/VF09.htm, Accessed January 11, 2022.

Principal Named for new South City Catholic Academy April 5, 2017, https://www.stlsouthcitycatholicacademy.org/blog/2017/4/5/new-principal-announced, Accessed December 14, 2021.

Record Exchange, http://www.recordexchangestl.com/, Accessed December 13, 2021.

St. Louis County Missouri Tilles Park https://stlouiscountymo.gov/st-louis-county-departments/parks/places/tilles-park/ Accessed December 14, 2021.

St. Louis Streets Index (1994) http://rbsc.slpl.org/STL_STREETS_(A-Z).pdf, Accessed February 17, 2022.

Slyman, Bobby, interview, February 15, 2016.

Tilles Park, Overview and amenities for Tilles Park, https://www.stlouis-mo.gov/government/departments/parks/parks/browse-parks/view-park.cfm?parkID=88&parkName=Tilles%20Park, Accessed December 14, 2021.

Young, Rhonda, interview February 16, 2016.

The End of the Road

Archdiocese of St. Louis, Closed Parishes https://www.archstl.org/archdiocesan-archives/closed-parishes, Accessed December 28, 2021.

Central Visual & Performing Arts High School, https://www.slps.org/cvpa, Accessed: June 21, 2022.

City of St. Louis, City Charter, https://www.stlouis-mo.gov/government/city-laws/charter/index.cfm, Accessed August 17, 2022.

Collegiate School of Medicine and Bioscience, https://www.slps.org/Page/17292, Accessed: June 21, 2022.

Family Search website, https://www.familysearch.org/en/ Accessed June 13, 2022.

St. Louis Neighborhoods, The Hill, by Norbury Wayman, https://www.stlouis-mo.gov/archive/neighborhood-histories-norbury-wayman/thehill/index13.htm, Accessed December 28, 2021 and other dates.

Bilyeu, Kathleen, interview, June 7, 2022.

Missouri Department of Mental Health, St. Louis Forensic Treatment Center, https://dmh.mo.gov/ftc, Accessed June 8, 2022 St. Louis Forensic Treatment Center.

The 1953 Great St. Louis Bank Robbery, https://kenzimmermanjr.com/great-st-louis-bank-robbery/, Accessed December 30, 2021, February, 8, 2022.

Overview and amenities for Sublette Park, https://www.stlouis-mo.gov/government/departments/parks/parks/browse-parks/view-park.cfm?parkID=83&parkName=Sublette+Park, Accessed December 28, 2021.

Peakbagger.com, Sublette Park Hill, Missouri, https://www.peakbagger.com/peak.aspx?pid=6569, Accessed Dec. 28, 2021.

Topographic-Map.com, https://en-us.topographic-map.com/maps/kfp/St-Louis/, Accessed December 28, 2021.

Truman Restorative Center Demolished, http://preservationresearch.com/demolition/truman-center/, Accessed: August 13, 2022.

1883 MacAdam Report, https://www.towergrovepark.org/macadam

Merkel, Jim, Hoosiers and Scrubby Dutch, St. Louis, Mo, Reedy Press, 2014.

Hunyar, Amanda, St. Louis State Hospital: A 150-Year Journey Toward Hope. 2019 Reedy Press St. Louis

St. Louis Chronic Hospital, https://www.asylumprojects.org/index.php?title=St._Louis_Chronic_Hospital, Accessed, August 17, 2022.

Southwest Bank Robbery July 23, 2012, https://www.stltoday.com/news/multimedia/southwest-bank-robbery-1953/image_f2867c82-dd14-57e0-bc93-d977462b4986.html, Accessed Feb. 8, 2022.

St. Louis Magazine A Tour of the Sites Highlighted in "St. Louis Modern" https://www.stlmag.com/history/a-tour-for-the-sites-highlighted-in-st-louis-modern/ Accessed December 27, 2021.

Epilogue

Allrecipes, Green salad, https://www.allrecipes.com/recipe/14452/green-salad/, Accessed October 27, 2022.

Facebook conversation between author and Karen Baer, October 16-17, 2022.

The author's neighbors, Harry, Dot and Clayton and Don.

Oldenburg, Ray The Great Good Place: Cafes, Coffee Shops, Bookstores, Bars, Hair Salons and Other Hangouts at the Heart of the Community. New York: Marlowe and Company, 1989.

Stl-Style https://www.stl-style.com/

Vines, Randy, email to author.